BLUE MAN
IN A
RED STATE

**Montana's Governor Brian Schweitzer
and the New Western Populism**

Greg Lemon

Foreword by Former U.S. Representative Pat Williams

TWODOT®

GUILFORD, CONNECTICUT
HELENA, MONTANA
AN IMPRINT OF THE GLOBE PEQUOT PRESS

A · T W O D O T® · B O O K

Text design by Maggie Peterson

Library of Congress Cataloging-in-Publication Data
Lemon, Greg.
  Blue man in a red state : Montana's Governor Brian Schweitzer and the new western populism / Greg Lemon.
    p. cm.
  ISBN 978-0-7627-4494-7
1. Schweitzer, Brian, 1955– 2. Governors—Montana—Biography.
3. Democratic Party (Mont.)—Biography. 4. Montana—Politics and government. 5. Populism—Montana. 6. West (U.S.)—Politics and government. 7. Populism—West (U.S.) 8. Democratic Party (U.S.) I. Title.
  F735.2.S38L46 2008
  978.6'034092—dc22
  [B]

                                                    2008015847

Printed in the United States of America

10 9 8 7 6 5 4 3 2 1

To Renee
For loving my dreams

Contents

Foreword

by Pat Williams

Montana's Governor Brian Schweitzer came into Montana politics while our state and this region are in renaissance. Perhaps the West's changing landscape is even more interesting than this colorful and intelligent governor.

One of America's great poets, Bob Dylan, could have been describing today's Rocky Mountain West when he wrote, "The times, they are a-changing." From the high deserts of the Southwest to the soaring peaks and rolling plains of the Northern Rockies, the West is in the midst of a historic transition. In our economics and politics we are not what we were. We all recognize, of course, that the Wild West's days of massive cattle drives, homestead stampedes, and buffalo slaughter ended suddenly a long time ago. The current transition that has been occurring for several decades is more subtle but every bit as historic as that original closing of the Old West.

Economic boom and bust was the hallmark of the states of the Rockies through the 1800s and until the mid-1980s. During the early years of that period the extraction of the region's natural resources was unabated. What seemed good for the economy was disastrous for the environment. An alarmed public caused governments, most notably the federal government, to respond beginning in the mid-1900s, with the 1960s and on becoming the decades of environmental consciousness and repair.

For the past three decades economic opportunities in the Rockies have been created not by extraction but rather through commercial and housing development, high-tech enterprises, services, and recreation. Unlike our past when people chased jobs, today's West is driven by an amenities economy in which jobs chase people and the people locate near the most attractive landscapes.

Our politics, too, are undergoing a significant transition: driven, in part by changes in resource extraction, particularly in these states here in the Northern Rockies. During the 1980s and '90s, political protests filled the Big Sky. Shovels to Nevada, Log Haul Rallies, and angry meetings made up the chainsaw politics of those who, understandably, were resisting the inevitable dislocations caused by price changes in the new worldwide commodity marketplace. That, combined with unemployment caused primarily through the increased productivity of new and more efficient machinery, meant fewer jobs for the workers but increased profits for the companies.

The 1980s Sagebrush Rebellion of a militant few was financed by the extractive industries, using as its foot soldiers disgruntled and out-of-work westerners. The federal government and often Democrats were cited as conducting a "War on the West." And that effective campaign made a political difference throughout the states of the Rocky Mountain West.

For one hundred years the West's political pendulum had swung consistently between Democrats and Republicans. It had been that way throughout my lifetime, including in 1978 when I was elected to the U. S. House of Representatives from Montana's 1st Congressional District. Throughout the western states, voters, as they had for decades, were electing both liberals and conservatives to high offices.

In our neighboring state of Idaho, the two U.S. Senators were the liberal Frank Church and the conservative Jim McClure. Here in Montana we had chosen conservative governors such as Tim Babcock while electing liberal Senators Mike Mansfield and Lee Metcalf to Washington, D.C.

However, nine terms and eighteen years later when I concluded my congressional career in 1997 and returned to Montana, arch-conservatives held a significant majority of western congressional seats and each of the eight states of the Rockies had a Republican governor.

Now twelve years later, the pendulum has swung again—five of our eight states have Democratic governors. Democrats hold a clear majority of the mayors and chief executives of our larger cities. Our state legislatures are closely balanced. More and more progressives are being elected to Congress.

It is into that transition that Montanans elected Brian Schweitzer. He fits our changing economic and political landscape. Neither all liberal, conservative, nor populist, Schweitzer has been able to stride the fault lines of our changing western landscape.

Acknowledgments

This book couldn't have been possible without the consistent and willing help of two people in Governor Schweitzer's office: his communications director Sarah Elliott, and his scheduler Cory Johns. They made the effort to accommodate every request for time and material. Chuck Johnson, capital bureau chief for Lee Newspapers in Montana, was also an incredible source of insight and information. He was always willing to spend an hour bouncing around ideas. Pat Williams and Bob Brown, both at the O'Connor Center for the Rocky Mountain West, provided essential background and context for the current state of Montana politics. Their perspective was invaluable to the development of this book. And of course my editor, Allen Jones. His incredible faith in me and his work on this project can't go without acknowledgment. Thank you all.

1

In the Governor's Office

"Remember when you told me I ought to write a book?"

I thought Montana's governor looked a little nonplussed. "Yeah . . ." he said, stalling.

We were sitting at a boardroom table in his office, a corner space on the second floor of the Capitol in Helena. The office was decorated with original Western paintings and bronzes, toy windmills, and conspicuous vials of synthetic fuel. A bag of Spitz sunflower seeds was on a table behind his desk.

"Well, I'd like to write a book about you."

In the months ahead I would find Brian Schweitzer a hard guy to surprise. Like most talented politicians he's usually one step ahead, anticipating a line of thought, the agenda behind a reporter's question. He keeps control of an interview. But I'd made him blink.

After a long moment he said, "You want to know what you should write a book about?" He leaned back in his chair, crossing his cowboy boots. "What the big issue in Montana is? Coal into fuel." And then he launched into another well-rehearsed lecture on Montana's coal-to-fuel potential. Again, I heard the layperson's explanation of how you press coal long and hard enough to release gas, which is then separated from carbon dioxide, refined, and burned by diesel engines. This process was Schweitzer's hobbyhorse and one on which he was hanging his political hat. To the extent that he had attracted international press attention, this was why. Being a journalist in Montana, I already had the whole thing down pat, as he had to know. Nevertheless, he went on.

Fifteen minutes later, I tried to steer the conversation back to politics. "Has the oil crisis helped turn the tide for Democrats in the West?"

"Has the tide turned, do you think?"

"I'd say so. And you seem to be at the front of it. I think that's why a book outlining that change and your political career might be timely."

"You know there's going to be a book about Jag," he said, pointing to the border collie at his feet. Another writer was working on a children's book about a day in the life of his dog. Schweitzer beamed like a proud parent.

Finally, with a part of his mind having clearly explored a separate track even while we were talking, he said, "Sure, we can work on a book together."

Pinning Schweitzer down can be tricky. As a journalist I expect politicians to keep me at a distance, but Schweitzer is naturally warmer. When I was a daily reporter and he called, I'd pick up the phone to hear, "How ya doin', cowboy? This is Brian Schweitzer." His interviews are quick and to the point. He loves to talk about his ideas. It's often difficult to steer interviews onto topics I'm probing. He likes to talk about what's on his mind, whether I need to know or not. Keeping him on track is a little like trying to catch a trout with your bare hands.

He's a big man. That's something all reporters seem to point out. He's nearly six foot three inches, and 215 pounds. I've never seen him wear anything but jeans and boots, usually with a sport coat and a blue shirt. The bolo tie came along after he got elected.

CNN reporter Candy Crowley called him the "Rock Star from the Rockies"; Mark Sundeen in the *New York Times Magazine* suggested he was a political "expert or virtuoso, or perhaps, a natural." The *Wall Street Journal* summed him up as having a "well-spoken, gun-owning, dog-loving, native-ritual-doing, shot-of-whiskey-drinking true-west style." His personality, on a national stage, is polished to a mirror shine, catnip to reporters who can't get enough of a politician who speaks his mind, who resists stereotypes.

To say Schweitzer burst onto the Montana political scene is somewhat of an understatement. He came out of nowhere in 2000 to challenge incumbent Republican senator Conrad Burns, losing by only a few percentage points. During this campaign he showed an early talent for political showmanship, making national news when he bussed seniors into Canada for prescription drugs. His near success at toppling Burns positioned him within his party for a run at the governor's office, which he won in 2004.

Before that? Well in 1993 he'd been appointed by Secretary of the Interior Alphonso Espy to sit on the Montana USDA Farm Service Agency Committee. He was also appointed to the sixteen-member National Drought Task Force in 1999. Both positions were probably evidence of some early political maneuvering, although he resists the idea. Prior to being governor, he'd held no elected office. Yet sharing the spotlight with his dog Jag and having a populist's instinct for appealing to his constituency, Schweitzer has managed to recast the political dialogue, not only in Montana but across the Rocky Mountain West.

Although he's arguably the most dynamic politician Montana has produced in recent history, his lack of experience sometimes shows. His supporters will sometimes shake their heads good-naturedly at his gaffes while his detractors will say he's "all hat, no cattle." He likes to present himself as bipartisan, however under his watch Montana's political landscape has remained contentious. Schweitzer's popularity (sometimes exceeding 70 percent) points to his appeal with Democrats and Independents, but hard-line Republicans point to his partisan rhetoric and big spending. Democrats like to talk about how, under

Schweitzer's leadership, they've cut taxes, improved education, and increased energy production. And when it comes to bridge building, he did pick a Republican running mate. He can talk as fast as an auctioneer about energy development, and if he thinks you're falling asleep, well, he's got his vials of synthetic diesel, a visual aid even the most distracted farmer is not likely to forget. He takes his role as an energy educator very seriously.

As a reporter who leans toward being a middle ground Independent, I'm biased in favor of someone who plows his own ground. But my questions about Schweitzer loom large. Is this persona—the dog, the blue jeans, the bolo tie, the boots—all an act? Does he really believe in himself this much? Is there a key, a Rosetta stone, that will explain the bravado, the ego? Has he set his sights on the national arena, or is he content, as he has so often implied, with state office? Is he truly concerned about Montana? Does he really want to change the world?

Schweitzer has a way of winning people over. When you shake his hand and he grins, it's impossible not to grin back. If he lets his guard down and tells a few stories, they're usually laced with cussing and knee slapping. It's tough to remain objective. We talk fishing every chance we get, and while I'm still not sold on his skills with a fly rod, there's no doubt he's one of the most talented politicians to ever ride the governor's chair in Montana.

If the past is any indication of the future, Brian Schweitzer is on course to becoming one of the most influential Montana politicians since Mike Mansfield.

But who is he?

2

First Impressions

I first met Brian Schweitzer at a campaign rally in Montana's Bitterroot Valley in the fall of 2004. I was the environmental reporter for a small daily newspaper in Hamilton, assigned to cover the rally due to our small staff.

Schweitzer was the new darling of his party and, at the time, well ahead in the polls. His opponent, Republican secretary of state Bob Brown, wasn't proving to be the contender that conservatives around Montana had hoped. At the time Schweitzer was leading Brown in most polls by a solid twenty points. Schweitzer told people not be fooled by the polls. He knew it was going to tighten up as Election Day closed in, and he was right. (He eventually won by only five points.) He kept running a shrewdly effective series of campaign ads that frequently featured him on horseback, often with a gun. The message that he kept repeating in a dozen different subtle ways was that he was one of us. He was a regular guy.

Schweitzer's campaign was all about energy and attitude, particularly in contrast to his opponent. Bob Brown is an engaging but quiet guy, not in any way flashy or boisterous. Not one to wade through a crowd shaking hands and slapping backs, he's smart and studious but staid. Put him next to Schweitzer and it's like seeing a Lutheran minister sitting beside Axl Rose.

Although Schweitzer was running late, the small bar in Hamilton was open and the red wine and microbrew were flowing. Then everyone's head turned toward the door. Through the crowd, over the rows of baseball caps and cowboy hats, Montana's Democratic candidate for governor entered, wearing blue jeans, boots, and a sport coat. Nothing fancy, nothing to really set him apart, but there was no doubt who the star was. Shaking hands, grinning, Schweitzer pushed into the crowded room. A cheer rose from the fringes and found its way toward the center of the room.

A few minutes went by before I had a chance to shake hands and introduce myself as a journalist from conservative Ravalli County. He turned, oblivious to the dozens of faces turned his way, and talked to me about the weather. It was a fair day, and he had spent it walking around Hamilton, meeting business owners and employees, even getting a haircut. A rare thing for him, his hands were shoved in his jeans pockets. They're usually waving around as he tells a story. He rocked back and forth, heel to toe, in his cowboy boots.

I wasn't all that sure what to expect from Schweitzer. I'd heard rumors sifting down from Helena. "He's charismatic," said Marshall Bloom, local director of the Rocky Mountain Laboratories and a rabid Hamilton Democrat. "Wait until you meet him."

My first impression, however, was that he seemed uncomfortable. He stood aside from the crowd to talk weather with a local reporter but didn't really engage the audience, not until he was called to the microphone. Then his charisma emerged.

"I speak from the heart," he had just told me. And now as the crowd cheered and hollered, Schweitzer addressed them without notes.

He talked about how he'd traveled to all fifty-six Montana counties, meeting people, listening to ideas. Standard political road show stuff, of course, but Schweitzer was taking it to a new level. He'd helped change a

First Impressions

flat on the side of the highway and had coffee in small restaurants across eastern Montana. He was, he said, just visiting with the people, listening. No script, no plan, no notes.

As a way of introducing himself to the crowd in Hamilton, Schweitzer launched into a football story.

As a freshman, Schweitzer went to Geyser High School. It is a rural school, too small even to field a regular eleven-man football team. They played eight-man. Like almost every other male student, Schweitzer went out for the team, despite being on the small side. Their first game of the season was rival and eight-man powerhouse, Belt High School. "They breed their boys big over in Belt," Schweitzer laughed. "And the opposing linemen looked like college studs rather than farm boys."

Schweitzer was the third-string quarterback and began the game on the bench. But the starting quarterback was eaten alive by the Belt defensive line on the first play of the game. The backup was Geyser's star running back. He was knocked out of the game in the next play. So the coach turned to the small, skinny freshman on the bench.

Schweitzer said he went out to the huddle without knowing really what to do. He kneeled down in the group of players and looked up at them expectantly. "Well," he said, "I'm listening. What should we do?"

The parallels, of course, were clear. It was analogous of what he was doing all around Montana at the time—looking to the citizens and asking for their advice and ideas.

I watched the crowd. They were captivated. It was a story I was to hear a few times during Schweitzer's race and always to great effect. But was Schweitzer really saying that he was still a scared third-string kid clueless about the next play? Was he really looking for advice on what his priorities should be? One could hardly believe that he'd run for office without already having a sense for what he hoped to accomplish.

In the months after Schweitzer took office, however, it became clear that this was a fairly typical way for him to engage the public, an instinctive and shrewd nod to our appetite for narrative. Sure, a football

7

story that made him look like a naïve weakling was an unexpected way to relate to voters, but telling stories is Schweitzer's style. It's something he's become a master at. And this particular story humanized him, made him one of us.

The story could also serve as a spot of humility in Schweitzer. As I discovered, he believes Montanans are tired of hearing politicians tell them what's best for their lives. So with a football story, he was telling people he would listen to, and value, their ideas. He wanted them to understand that even though he was running for the top elected position in the state, he was still just a regular Montanan at heart. As much as any political agenda, that seems to be one of Brian Schweitzer's most urgent goals. He wants to be one of us.

3

Not Your Typical
Democrat

"He is the best politician I've seen since I've been in politics," said Jim Shockley, a salty Republican state senator from Victor, a small town in the Bitterroot Valley. "He's very good on his feet. He's personable. He knows people. He knows how the system works."

Schweitzer's charisma keeps spilling over the brim. It keeps people listening, even if they are looking for a mistake to pounce on. Mike Cooney, the 2007 Montana senate president, recalls a luncheon he attended with Schweitzer, hosted by the Montana Broadcasters Association. Cooney expects the attendees were looking for Schweitzer to talk about the media or some other related subject. Instead he gave a speech on energy production in Montana, producing vials of biodiesel and synthetic fuel from his pockets. The audience was enthralled, even though they'd all likely heard some form of the speech before. Again, Schweitzer spoke with no notes, just energy. "I've never really heard him make a talk that didn't elicit a lot of discussion and feedback from the audience," Cooney said.

Schweitzer's energy gets him up at four in the morning perusing newspapers, calling staff, strategizing his next move. He told me he needs only four or five hours of sleep a night. John Bohlinger, his lieutenant governor, lived with Schweitzer for a period in Helena right after they took office and vouches for the energy.

"He just charges hard all day and doesn't stop for lunch," Bohlinger said.

New Mexico's Bill Richardson has that type of political drive, said Charles Mahtesian, editor of *The Almanac of American Politics*. So did Bill Clinton. "They're people who are just larger than life in all of their appetites." They have a work ethic beyond the high-powered stockbrokers of Wall Street, beyond the multi-billion-dollar CEOs in America. They're the kind of politicians that put two hundred thousand miles on their cars, crisscrossing their states to meet with voters, Mahtesian said. For Schweitzer, and politicians like him, it's about doing whatever it takes to succeed in the public venue of politics. It's a "No Doorbell Left Behind" attitude. "Democrats love politicians like [Schweitzer]," he said. "He has tremendous retail politicking skills. His fund-raising base is now national."

The energy he brought to his campaign didn't stop after he won the office. In an interview during the 2007 legislative session, Schweitzer told me, "No one outworks me. No one."

He's continued to crisscross the state, meeting with county commissioners and constituents. This has undoubtedly contributed to his popularity with voters. It's easy to like a governor if you've shaken hands with him and seen him in your local newspaper visiting with schoolkids and local elected leaders. Schweitzer himself estimates he's met 25 percent of Montanans—an astounding number, even for a politician like him.

On the other hand, some have said he's a polarizing figure. Is that fair? It's a notion that would no doubt raise his hackles. Having the luxury of taking office while Montana was still on the rebound from one of its historically most unpopular governors, Republican Judy Martz, he presented himself to voters as a bridge builder, a politician beyond Montana's inner circle, an average Montanan who would listen to his constituents and take their ideas to Helena.

Even some in his own party look at his dealings with Republicans and cringe a little. Democratic state senator Jim Elliott believes Schweitzer is a good politician but hasn't done a lot to build bridges with the Republicans. "If being in the legislature has taught me anything, it is that personal relationships are more important in politics than anything else. You have to develop the ability to disagree—even violently disagree— with someone who's a friend."

But Cooney defends Schweitzer. "I think bipartisanship is just having the ability to work with both sides . . . Get people to the table and you're eventually finally able to convince them of the merit of the position you're trying to promote." In his estimation, Schweitzer's been able to do that in key instances.

But at times Republican leadership in Montana has been simply unwilling to come to the table. It seems like it might be hard to build a bridge when the other side keeps blowing up their end. Schweitzer clearly isn't your typical Democrat. Like most of his peers in the Democrat Party in the Rocky Mountain West, he supports gun ownership, comes out strong in favor of private property rights, is apt to quote Bible verses in public forums, and has become known for a certain kind of fiscal caution. In September 2007 he called the legislature back for a special session to fund the cost of fighting another bad year of wildfires. Many Republicans questioned why he would call the session before the fire season was over, but Schweitzer dismissed their concerns. A good business, he said, pays its bills on time. Montana wasn't going to run up a debt when it had money in the bank, not under his watch. He sees coal development as the financial key to Montana's future and pursues it with a persistence that can seem at times single-minded. The cowboy boots and jeans are permanent fixtures no matter the venue, whether he's talking at the National Press Club, being interviewed by Charlie Rose, or tossing one back at the M&M in Butte. A Democrat, yes, but one who believes that big government doesn't mean good government. He knows that people in Montana would rather be left alone. He understands frivolous taxes aren't popular, but the Republican establishment in Washington, D.C., has left the average family struggling to find ways to pay for health insurance, housing, and gas for their cars.

As opposed to most other politicians in the national arena, he can talk to farmers about diversifying their crop portfolios and fishermen about hatches on the Missouri River. A master of the ten-second sound bite, he conducts the press like an orchestra, but consistently says he has the people of Montana at heart. He never misses a chance to get out and shake hands with citizens, a bottle of Purell Hand Sanitizer in his pocket.

As a politician, and as evidenced by the nature of the criticism he's drawn, he's devoted to his causes. For example, Roy Brown, state house Republican leader in the 2005 legislative session (and gubernatorial candidate for 2008), publicly took him to task for threatening legislators who might vote against his initiatives. Brown said Schweitzer was telling Republican freshman legislators that he would campaign against them in the next election if they didn't support his bills supporting ethanol, wind energy, and ethics reform. "I've never heard of a governor who used the bully pulpit of his office to do that kind of thing to an individual freshman legislator," Brown told Lee Newspaper reporter Allison Farrell. "It's just not proper."

Schweitzer didn't actually deny the complaints, but his spokesperson, Sarah Elliott, said the governor was concerned with doing what was best for the people of Montana, and that the accusations of threats were silly. Indeed, the behavior Brown described would look to Schweitzer supporters like evidence of a passionate commitment to his principles, not abuse of his "bully pulpit." It's all in the ideology of the beholder.

4

Montana

Mountains to the west and plains to the east, Brian Schweitzer, like all Montanans, may best be described by the landscape he calls home. If you live in a rural county like Petroleum or Garfield, your closest neighbor might be miles away. If you're in one of the state's urban centers, however, you've been seeing growth rates of 2 to 5 percent a year. Montana's population is mostly held in an L shape from Kalispell south through Missoula and then east to Billings, with an anomaly in Great Falls. This portion of the state is seeing the most growth. The population of the rest is either stagnating or shrinking. These extremes give the state a confusing sense of identity. Out in the country, neighbors are leaving, and schools are consolidating, while in Bozeman, Missoula, and Kalispell, Montanans have traffic jams going to work.

The history of Europeans in Montana, like most of the West, is as thin as Rocky Mountain topsoil. You don't have to scrape too deep to get to bedrock. Back in the 1860s and 1870s, the cattlemen from Texas started filtering in, spreading out through the eastern half of the state, fattening beeves on grass the likes of which they'd never seen. The buffalo herds were already starting their precipitous decline, shot into near oblivion by market hunters. The Crow and Blackfoot, Assiniboine Sioux and Northern Cheyenne, Shoshone and Nez Perce, and the Flathead and Gros Ventre were all in various states of decline, treated with greater or lesser degrees of violence and dishonesty.

After the cattlemen came the farmers, immigrating in droves from the upper Midwest and Europe, following the railroad and its propaganda, the claims that all it took to make your fortune was a horse, a plow, and a sack of seed. Finding less than twelve inches of precipitation a year, most of the homesteaders who broke ground on the dry plains were doomed to failure.

K. Ross Toole, in *Twentieth Century Montana: A State of Extremes,* writes about the amazing influx of homesteaders. "It is estimated that between 70,000 and 80,000 people flooded into eastern and central Montana between 1909 and 1918 and that at least 60,000 left by 1922. But that is an estimate. No one really knows, and the census is essentially mute."

In 1920 Musselshell County had 12,030 people. Today only about 4,500 Montanans call it home. Meanwhile, in 1950, Bozeman's Gallatin County had a population of around 22,000. Today, with its proximity to skiing, fly-fishing, and great expanses of wilderness, it's home to over 81,000. In 1990 the median home price in Bozeman was about $64,000. By 2003 the price had increased to $188,000. Four years later, in 2007, it was $279,300. (In a famous passage in her book, *The Legacy of Conquest,* historian Patricia Nelson Limerick wrote, "If Hollywood wanted to capture the emotional center of Western history, its movies would be about real estate. John Wayne would have been neither a gunfighter nor a sheriff, but a surveyor, speculator, or claims lawyer.")

Montana's first gold rush took place in 1862 in the town of Bannack, near the present-day town of Dillon. Subsequent strikes were made in Last Chance Gulch, which spawned the capital city of Helena, and Alder Gulch near Virginia City. Bannack, at its peak, had a population of more than a thousand. Today it is a ghost town and state park. Virginia City and the small towns surrounding it once had a combined population of 6,000. Beef to wheat, copper to recreation, only the commodities have changed.

This settlement of Montana (cattle, homesteading, then mining) foreshadowed a trend that persists today: Immigrants come to take what they can. People have always come into Montana looking to make a buck, to find their commodity. It isn't called the Treasure State for nothing.

Toole, in his 1959 book *Montana: An Uncommon Land,* wrote, "The Montana pattern has been brief, explosive, frenetic, and often tragic. The economic picture has often been one of exploitation, overexpansion, boom, and bust. The political scene has been equally extreme—from fiery, wide-open violence to apathetic resignation. . . . There is little or nothing moderate about the story of Montana. It has ricocheted violently down the corridor of possibilities. What is good in reasonable measure is often bad in full measure, and Montana has been a place of full measure."

On May 26, 1864, Abraham Lincoln officially established the Montana Territory, appointing Sidney Edgerton as first territorial governor. A Free-Soil Republican from Ohio and a former colonel in the Union Army, Edgerton served only two years before giving the mantle to Thomas Meagher, an eccentric Irish revolutionary and brigadier general. Meagher died a mysterious death in the Missouri River (drowned— murdered or perhaps only drunk), providing an inauspicious start to the office. After another eight territorial and twenty-two state governors, Brian Schweitzer, twenty-third to hold the office, occupies a seat that has historically had to deal with gold rushes and vigilantes, range wars and land speculators, and socialist miners and copper barons.

Yet Montana has rarely undergone a period of change as turbulent as it is seeing now. Call it the age of recreationalist immigration. The issues are access to public lands, water allocation, wildfires, health care, and education. In essence, how will the state make the transition from a largely rural, agricultural economy to one of dynamic growth and urbanization? Brian Schweitzer, like every politician in the region, is faced with the challenge of juggling a set of widely divergent interests.

The Montana Department of Natural Resource and Conservation, to take only one small instance, has been trying to find a way to fund fire suppression. Currently the legislature allocates money for buying fire engines and hiring personnel but doesn't provide money for suppression. Take a few severe fire seasons and add an explosion of unplanned growth with palatial homes often sited in heavy timber, and protecting residential areas during forest fires is becoming increasingly expensive and dangerous.

The perennial issue of water allocation is being aggravated by increased population. In Ravalli County, as in other areas in the state, claims to water in the Bitterroot River basin currently exceed the amount of water in the system. Montana has been trying to inventory surface water rights around the state, but the job is enormous. It's a process that began more than twenty years ago and may not be finished for another two decades. In the meantime thousands of personal wells are being drilled to accommodate new growth. Imagine a sixty-home subdivision built fifteen miles away from the nearest town, each home with its own well. The effect of this growth on surface water, or ground water for that matter, is as yet unknown, and significant legislation dealing with the issue has yet to be passed.

The issue of public access is also rearing its ugly head. As traditional working ranches are bought for recreation rather than production, as No Trespassing signs begin to bloom, a true sense of community seems to be becoming a thing of the past. Montana streams that are open by state law (the water belongs to the public, so once a fisherman is in a river or stream, he can go where he wants within the high-water marks) are, almost every year, illegally closed off by landowners. In the 2007 legislative session, a bill was introduced that would have legally formalized access from public bridges, but it was defeated in the house along party lines, with Republicans voting against it.

If you're a politician in Montana, you face the issue of how to create legislation that will help alleviate these problems in the best interests of the state and, just as importantly, how to do it in such a way as to keep your polling numbers up. It's a daunting task. And yet, with approval ratings consistently in the high sixties and low seventies, Brian Schweitzer seems to be figuring it out.

5

The Populist

Schweitzer has been called a "prairie populist." In some ways, it's an easy label to hang on him, but one that's perhaps not entirely accurate.

Populism, to define it with a broad stroke, elevates the rights of individuals over businesses or corporations. Montana populists have historically been bent on reforming labor and mine-safety laws, and they've been interested in women's suffrage and the direct election of senators (U.S. Senators were elected by state legislatures until the 17th Amendment to the Constitution was passed in 1913.) As a party they were at their most powerful in the early twentieth century.

John Morrison and Catherine Wright Morrison, in their book, *Mavericks: The Lives and Battles of Montana's Political Legends,* wrote, "Montana's first populist movement grew up around dissatisfaction with territorial conditions and the consequent cry for statehood. The white male voters that peopled Montana before 1890 were recalcitrant spirits who ... teased and despised the eastern 'dudes' that Washington's Republican presidential administrations imposed upon them."

In populist fashion Schweitzer has championed land access for hunters and fishermen, gone to bat to freeze college tuition, and tried unsuccessfully to close what he calls tax loopholes, which, according to the governor, allow out-of-state corporations to elude paying their share of state taxes. Schweitzer's also pushed unsuccessfully for ethics reform in Helena. (He would like to limit the ability of politicians to leave office and step immediately into the role of lobbyist.) He's also publicly railed against out-of-state landowners who, he says, are buying up land in Montana and shutting out the public.

A cynic would say that Schweitzer's positions more accurately reflect his sharp reading of public sentiment as much as his earnest intention to promote change. Out-of-state landowners have, in some very prominent cases, tried to limit public access, but they have also funded local charities and conservation efforts. For instance, the Stock Farm Club, a gated development built in Ravalli County by investment mogul Charles Schwab, established the Greater Ravalli Foundation. Its focus is on providing college scholarships for local teenagers, food and clothing for low-income children, and school supplies for local teachers. On the conservation side, in 2007 Roger Lang, a former Silicon Valley CEO, placed his eleven-thousand-acre Sun Ranch, located in the Madison Valley near Yellowstone National Park, under a conservation easement. The easement protected a large expanse of critical elk, wolf, and grizzly bear habitat.

Schweitzer is certainly smart enough to see both sides of these issues. But as a third-generation Montanan, he's also in sync with his electorate. Montanans still have their suspicions of the "eastern dudes," and he knows it.

National reporters, those who have met him, talk about his bolo tie, blue jeans, and "gilded" silver belt buckle. But he likes to describe himself as a good listener. "All the time, I move and shift based on new information that I gain," Schweitzer said. "I'm very good at developing irrigation and crops. I'm world class. Everything else I'm a work in progress. I'm listening to what people have to say about issues, about places, about objects."

Schweitzer pointed to his support of all-day kindergarten. He ran for governor intending to provide more support for higher education, particularly community colleges and technical schools. But once in office he began listening to educators who said that early education was vital. So he shifted his position a little and put more money in kindergarten. "I didn't know that before. I didn't believe that before, but I do now."

But how did his populist image emerge? Three years into his administration, his personality and history are still enigmas. Numerous times in interviews with his associates, I was told that a person hadn't even heard of Schweitzer until he ran against Burns in 2000. Some of his biggest supporters didn't even really know what he was doing before then. One of his cabinet members, Mary Sexton—whom Schweitzer appointed to head the Montana Department of Natural Resources and Conservation in 2004—said that she believed she'd been in 4-H with one of Schweitzer's brothers.

He's one of the most popular governors in Montana's history and yet no one seems to know much at all about him.

6

The Roots of a Governor

In Montana, as across the Rocky Mountain West, a certain kind of legitimacy arises from a person's nativity. "Where you from?" is a question that can either earn you a pat on the back or make you the butt of a joke. Pull up to almost any stoplight, Missoula to Wolf Point, and you are likely to see a bumper sticker in the shape of Montana, the word "Native" superimposed. It's not really surprising, then, that Brian Schweitzer takes great pride in being a third-generation Montanan.

His parents, Adam and Kay, were both children of homesteaders. His father's family came to America from Germany by way of Russia, homesteading at the turn of the twentieth century, first in North Dakota and then near the small village of Goldstone, Montana, east of the Rocky Mountain Front. They were drawn by the promise of an irrigation project on the Milk River, but when the project failed to materialize, they raised their crops on dry land, irrigated by prayers and rain. Goldstone is a ghost town now, though you can still find the old homesite if you look hard enough.

Adam Schweitzer and his family survived the Depression to enjoy profitability in the 1940s. Like so many other homesteaders who lasted, they bought up the abandoned farms around them, patching together a spread. Adam came back from World War II and married Kay McKernan, whom he met at a dance. Kay's family came from Ireland to homestead outside of Box Elder, south of Havre, about the same time the Schweitzers settled in Goldstone. She was nineteen when they married and Adam was twenty-seven. They settled on the Schweitzer family farm and began raising kids. Their first three children were born while they lived on the farm in Goldstone. In 1955, while Kay was pregnant with Brian, they bought a ranch near Geyser, south of Havre and east of Great Falls. This was their leap into the cattle business.

Schweitzer describes his parents as opposites: Adam as quiet, reflective, and reserved, and Kay as more outgoing and optimistic. "She's Irish. He's German. I guess that's the math," he said.

Describing the differences between the two, as is Schweitzer's habit, he gave an example. If Adam is presented with a challenge, he looks at it from four key points: "I don't know how to do it; I don't have the tools to do it; there's not a book on how to do it; and it's never been done before — I'm not sure we can get it done." But Kay, he said, is different: "My mother would look at something and just say I think we can do that."

Kay has been the energy in the family. "She's outgoing. She's really the spark plug, always pushing to get to the next place and the next thing. She's very competitive and raised her children to be very competitive," Schweitzer said. "She's never been one who thought that, even though she's the child of an immigrant and doesn't have a high school education, that there should be anything she or her children couldn't do."

Schweitzer says he takes something from both of his parents. "In some ways I'm the manifestation of both. I look at things and say, 'Well, I think we can do that. I guess I'll try to do that. Now, I understand there's some challenges along the way and I don't have the tools and no one's done it before and there's not a book on how to do it, but, shoot, that doesn't mean we can't do it.' "

Schweitzer may have inherited a certain measure of his populism from his father. Adam was involved in the National Farmers Organization, a group founded in 1955 that focused on helping farmers get fair prices for their commodities. He served on the organization's national board of directors. There was a particular focus on monopolization from food processors, the control that allowed them to dictate markets. Brian Schweitzer said, "There is more concentration among food processors than any other industry in America." The NFO worked with farmers to gain more leverage when bargaining for prices.

The idea of championing the small guy is a Schweitzer family value Brian carries on. From small businesses to Montana farmers and ranchers, and local hunters and fishermen fighting against out-of-state landowners—Schweitzer talks often of going to bat for the little guy, for "the last and the least."

7

Across the West

Schweitzer calls it "The Blue Highway," —a strip of liberal governorships from Montana through Wyoming and down to Colorado, New Mexico, and Arizona. This ascendancy of Democratic governors, with Schweitzer in the vanguard, have been able to court conservative and moderate voters by taking on issues Democrats had previously ceded to the Republicans.

In an article for *Time* magazine, Joe Klein wrote, "Something strange and tangy is happening in the Rocky Mountains. The Democratic Party is being reborn, with a raft of colorful candidates who have won the hearts of independents and moderate Republican voters."

Klein maintains that the top-tier Democratic presidential candidates are coming off overly liberal and urban, traits that have never played well with Rocky Mountain voters. "At a time when political pomp and blab have come to seem prohibitively pompous and bloviational, Rocky Mountain politics is fresh and innovative and fun. It might not be a bad idea for Hillary and Barack and the rest to pause for a moment . . . and take a look at what's happening just west of Iowa, in an electorally overlooked region of the country that just may hold the key to winning the White House in 2008."

Democrats in the Rocky Mountains have found success by being pragmatic and moderate, he wrote. This has meant finding real solutions to issues vital to the region: energy, growth, conservation, natural resources, and immigration. Democratic governors in the region are lowering taxes and coming up with innovative ways to address the demand for alternative energy. "Democrats also tend to reflect a Western live-and-let-live attitude on social issues like abortion and homosexuality. But given the traditional Western aversion to lockstep conformity, none of the above are hard-and-fast rules," he wrote.

Brian Schweitzer, not unlike his populist peers, has a portfolio of positions that more accurately reflect the varied tastes of his constituency than cater to his party. In terms of gun control, he has said, "You take care of your guns; I'll take care of mine." With regard to gay marriage, Schweitzer told Charlie Rose that, while Montana recently passed a constitutional amendment defining marriage as between a man and woman, it's not that simple: "Montana is a libertarian place. Keep the government off our back, out of our bedroom—we don't want to hear from you unless we need you."

When Rose pressed him on how he personally felt, Schweitzer balked, but did say, "We'll work on legal means for adults to live their lives together—civil union, something like that."

As opposed to some of his other counterparts—and further reflecting his constituency—Schweitzer embraces faith in a way that seems entirely unaffected. He graduated from high school in a Catholic abbey in Colorado. Taking care of the "last and the least" was something he learned in his youth from his parents. His family was always finding ways to aid those who were less fortunate. "We just always knew it was important to help people out," he said.

In his 2007 State of the State address, he quoted the Gospel of Matthew: "For a tree will be known by its fruits." This was meant as a challenge to the Montana legislature that was just beginning one of the most contentious sessions in recent history.

He has a way of appealing to both parties by refusing to look like either. He claims to be fiscally conservative, wanting to cut taxes as often as he can, but he is also proenvironment, to a point. He has said, "People are investing in places like Montana and Colorado and New Mexico because they want to live there." It becomes a quality-of-life issue, involving quantifiable resources like education and public health, but also intangibles like community and recreation. "We're going to protect their quality of life because we're going to maintain the quality of places for recreation," he told Rose.

However, that issue which is nearest and dearest to Schweitzer—coal development—introduces contradictions, both in terms of his views toward the environment (it will require strip mining, which has attracted criticism from the green lobby) as well as his specific agenda with regard to big corporations (he would like to see incentives in place to attract certain relevant industries to Montana). Not surprising, perhaps. For a state as dynamic and as imbued with contradictions as Montana, any reductive tag, be it "conservative" or "liberal," "Democrat" or "Republican," is going to only tell half the story.

8

Governors along the Blue Highway

In 2006 Rocky Mountain states, from Montana to New Mexico, all had Democratic governors—this in a region long thought by the rest of the nation to be conservative. Schweitzer's resonation in Montana is part of a larger trend in the region. These governors, like Schweitzer, have found success in the middle ground. Look at the state capital offices in New Mexico, Colorado, and Montana, and you'll find Democrats who consider themselves moderates.

Scratch the surface of these governors, and you'll find similarities in policies, almost like they are reading each other's game plans. Schweitzer is a trendsetter among these Rocky Mountain moderates, but New Mexico governor and former presidential candidate Bill Richardson came first.

Unlike Schweitzer, Richardson won the top spot in New Mexico with a long and distinguished political resume. He was a congressman in the 1980s, as well as U.S. secretary of energy and U.N. ambassador under the

Clinton administration. He's dealt with North Korea about nukes and sat across the table from Saddam Hussein. He is also partially of Hispanic decent, which could potentially appeal to a large voting block in not only New Mexico, but much of the West.

As governor of New Mexico, Richardson has pushed through policies for cleaner energy, tax incentives for the movie industry, better education (including all-day kindergarten), and lower taxes—all issues Schweitzer himself has championed.

In a 2005 article in *Salon*, former *Albuquerque Journal* reporter Shea Anderson profiled Richardson, who at the time was in the midst of a reelection bid in New Mexico. Anderson described a politician who is seemingly comfortable in the spotlight. He likes television cameras, aggressively promotes himself, and is extremely comfortable with the press. Anderson wrote, "Richardson has a knack for self-promotion that is more naked. In 2003, after the successful passage of a series of income-tax reductions, Richardson's administration took out a full-page ad in the *Wall Street Journal*, supposedly pitching New Mexico's positive business climate but also featuring a thoughtful Richardson. 'A Democrat cutting taxes?' the ad read. 'Things are different in New Mexico.' "

Richardson's self-promotion had many people in New Mexico thinking Richardson was looking for a higher office. "He said that for years [he wasn't looking for anything more] but everybody knew the day he was elected that the governorship was just a step for his presidential bid," said Emily Esterson, a journalist in New Mexico.

Despite his desire for a higher office, he made tough decisions as governor, such as pushing through a medical marijuana bill. Despite potential backlash Richardson said it was the right thing to do. He also pushed through a bill banning cockfighting, a hot issue in New Mexico, Esterson said. She wonders now if the bill wasn't an early nod toward his presidential run. It would look bad for a presidential candidate to be the governor of a state where something as crude as cockfighting was still legal.

He also pushed through initiatives to cut taxes for the film industry in hopes of attracting Hollywood to invest in the state. In fact, economic development in New Mexico has been a cornerstone of the Richardson administration, Esterson said.

But he's not been without controversy. Like Schweitzer, Richardson has been accused of being a bully. In the fall of 2007, a website was started, in part, as an outlet for people to document examples of Richardson's bullying behavior, according to an article in the *Albuquerque Journal*. The newspaper detailed accounts by several state employees who said they lost their jobs because they didn't fall in line with what the Richardson administration wanted.

Richardson spokesperson Gilbert Gallegos responded to some of the accusations: "The governor makes no apologies for holding employees and appointees accountable for their performance."

In a December 2005 article, the *Albuquerque Journal* outlined how Richardson was the subject of more controversy. The piece described his habit of joking with and touching people close to him, including his lieutenant governor, Diane Denish. Denish told the newspaper that Richardson would pinch her or touch "my hip, my thigh, sort of the side of my leg." She later said the comments were taken out of context, and she didn't feel the governor's behavior was inappropriate.

But Richardson has even been known to head-butt reporters during an interview or grab people in a headlock and ruffle their hair. Shea Anderson discussed this in a *Salon* piece. "I can recall at least two occasions in which Richardson flipped me the bird across a press conference table. Catching my eye as others spoke, he slowly put his middle finger up to his eye, as if to scratch an itch. It was like taking notes from a frat boy."

Richardson remains wildly popular in New Mexico. He won reelection in 2006 by 69 percent of the vote. Much like Schweitzer, he considers himself a man of the people and a good listener. Anderson describes Richardson "walking away from meetings with his pockets filled with scraps of paper people have given him. He collects them in plastic baggies and hands them to staff later, as problems for them to solve."

The newest moderate Democrat to become governor in the Rocky Mountain West is Colorado's Bill Ritter. Ritter was elected in 2006 with 56 percent of the vote. Like Richardson and Schweitzer, Ritter campaigned less on a party agenda and more on commonsense solutions to issues like education, health care, and energy. Ritter is a native Coloradoan and, like Schweitzer, grew up rural and poor. Ritter was one of twelve children, and his family lived on about five acres on the outskirts of Denver. His father was an alcoholic and left the family when Ritter was still young.

Ritter worked his way through college and earned a law degree from the University of Colorado. His only elected office before becoming governor was Denver district attorney. And he wasn't the first gubernatorial choice of the Democratic establishment in Colorado. Ritter's pro-life stance had many in the party worried, but he worked hard to meet with citizens around the state during the campaign. His stance on abortion was attributed to life experiences as a parent and missionary in Africa, as well as his Catholic faith. He stuck to his stance and in the end, according to *Denver Post* reporter Curtis Hubbard, people respected him for it.

Like Schweitzer, Ritter made it to all of the counties in Colorado during the campaign. Since being elected governor, he has made nearly one hundred trips outside the Denver area to engage with his electorate. Hubbard wrote, "People in Colorado like it when the government doesn't just exist in the capital city—when they bring it out on the plains and into the mountains. The governor has been there and tries to understand the issue on the ground."

Like Schweitzer, Ritter came into power with a sweeping majority in state government. For the first time in forty-four years, Democrats controlled the state house, the state senate, and the governor's office. Despite the luxury of party control, Ritter upset his fellow Democrats in February 2007 when he vetoed a hotly contested bill that would have unionized the state workforce. In his veto letter he sharply admonished the legislature for the partisan debate. "From the beginning, this was a bitter, divisive and partisan battle. Opposite sides dug in, refusing to consider reasonable compromises. It demonstrated precisely why so many people have grown so cynical about American politics. The bill's proponents made no effort to open a dialogue with the opponents. At times, the opponents were neither respectful nor civil. It was overheated politics at its worst."

Democrats were upset with the veto and Republicans were pleased. Then in November, Ritter issued an executive order establishing the right for state workers to unionize and bargain collectively. The executive order said the legislature and the governor would still have the right to set budgets, and it included a "no-strike" clause. The order, a watered-down version of the legislation he had vetoed, was privately complained about by unions. Ritter immediately experienced a swift and bitter backlash from Republicans, who claimed Ritter had essentially sold the state to the unions. The *Denver Post* even ran a front-page editorial claiming Ritter was a union "toady" and would likely be the first one-term governor in Colorado in decades.

However, despite the controversy, Ritter remains popular. In his first year he boasted popularity ratings of over 70 percent.

Like Schweitzer, Ritter has a progressive energy policy that includes cutting industrial greenhouse gasses, investing in alternative energy, and curbing auto emissions.

Still, like Montana, Colorado is experiencing a big energy boom with oil companies drilling new wells and bringing a lot of money into the state coffers. The trick for Ritter, again like other governors in the Rocky Mountain West, will be to see the benefit from oil and gas extraction while protecting natural resources and pushing a new energy agenda.

From New Mexico to Montana, these are offices defined by their success in reconciling the contradictions.

9

The Family Dynamic

Adam and Kay Schweitzer's six children came in twos. Darwin and Warren were born in 1947 and 1949. Five years later came Mike and Brian, a year and a half apart. Five years later came Walter and then Mary.

Neither Kay nor Adam finished high school, but they wanted more for their children. They realized that education provided the only real chance their children would have of living a life off the family ranch, and their children, including Brian, have all realized that dream. Darwin works as a farmer and realtor in Idaho and eastern Oregon. Warren and Mike both have careers in anesthesiology, Warren in California and Mike in Billings. Walter is a rancher and political strategist in Montana, and Mary makes her living as a business consultant in Cleveland, Ohio.

"Dad said, 'Look if you don't get an education, you're going to be doing this [labor on the ranch] the rest of your life.' And a lot of times that wasn't too appealing," Mike Schweitzer said. I interviewed Mike Schweitzer over the phone, and he sounds just like Brian. In fact, when he returned my call, if the caller ID hadn't shown a Billings number, I would have assumed it was the governor. Like his brother he has a sense of humor and speaks in a conversational way that leaves a lot of room for stories. He answered questions in a matter-of-fact way but elaborated without much prompting, much like Brian.

Even with the family's emphasis on education, some days the children were needed on the ranch and didn't go to school. But this was also an opportunity. Mike said, "We sometimes worked day and night, especially during calving season. There were a number of things that I think all of us learned and didn't really appreciate until much later."

The Schweitzers were always pushing, always aspiring. Their father, Adam, was one of the first ranchers in Montana to breed Simmental cattle, for instance. He also early on adopted the practice of impregnating cows by embryo transplants. In time the Schweitzers would be known for producing good bloodlines, showing their cattle at livestock events around the region. "Their whole life was a constant learning process," Mike said.

Adam Schweitzer was an accomplished mechanic. When he was young, his family bought one of the first tractors in the area. He was about the right age to be responsible for keeping it running. And after he had his own ranch and his children were running the equipment, his mechanical skills came in handy again.

The Schweitzers were a family of innovators and thinkers. All but two of Kay and Adam's children went on to get advanced degrees in college. According to Mike they were always encouraged to question things and not be afraid to think outside the box. "I learned over the years not to be surprised by anything Brian does," Mike said. "He's lived his whole life outside the box." On the farm Mike always did things the way his dad said. But Brian was different. "He was always looking for a better way to do the same things. Sometimes he found them and sometimes he got in trouble for not doing it right."

Mike remembers when Brian developed a better way of keeping the 4-H steers cool. In those days it was chic for the steers to have long hair when they were shown. Unfortunately the state fair in Great Falls was in August, the hottest part of the year in Montana. The accepted solution was to keep the steers in a dark barn and spray the sides of the barn with water to keep the inside cool. That barn had to be sprayed every couple of hours to keep the temperature down, a tedious chore.

So Brian decided to do something different. He rigged up a series of hoses and burlap sacks that would stay wet longer. Then he ran the hoses off of a water barrel so they didn't need constant attention. And it worked. "He didn't have to go out to the barn as often because the water was continuously running," Mike said.

Schweitzer claims he was born a deal maker and a thinker. It comes from being a middle child. "You are squeezed between the big and the little. From day one you're in a constant negotiation. You don't personally have the power, the juice to do anything. You're in the middle and you're a deal maker."

It was this family dynamic that, in hindsight, had the most influence on his leadership skills. "No one would ever point to me as being the fastest, the tallest, the shortest, the thinnest, the fattest, the quickest, the prettiest, the ugliest—I'm just a guy. So being just a guy, I use whatever I got and what I got is God-given and I thank God for that. But beyond that it is a constant honing of your skills and I suppose that sends you to leadership."

"In order for you to accomplish the most you have to bring people together. Some people call that leadership. I don't know, I call it deal making. The deal making means, if I'm going to accomplish something, I know that it's going to take more than my two hands and more than just the space between my two ears. It's going to take the creative skills of all the people around me and my ability to motivate them, entice them, reward them and if they're successful, I'll be successful. I think that's leadership."

The Schweitzer ranch was a family operation, and, though they made it work, they weren't rich. "We never thought we were poor," Mike Schweitzer said. "I think it's kind of funny when I look back on it now.

Relatively speaking we were very poor, yet my folks kept talking a lot of times that we should help other people who were really poor."

This philosophy certainly belies the family's deep Catholic faith. And it may also have to do with the knowledge that though they were getting by, one unlucky event could turn things grim. "We knew how tenuous it was," Mike said, "surviving out on the prairie."

Brian remembered one dry year when the crops just didn't come in. His parents sat the kids down and told them Christmas was going to be really slim. "But we've got to pull together," Adam and Kay told their kids.

As part of this pulling together, the family shared a faith that God ultimately had control. Summer thunderstorms can rage across central and eastern Montana, massacring crops with hail. Instead of buying crop insurance, however, the Schweitzers would more typically burn palm leaves in their wheat fields, sprinkle them with holy water, and pray for protection, a tradition Brian's grandmother, Francesca Schweitzer, brought from the old country.

In all it seemed like they had more bad years than good, but, according to Brian, they made it work through an optimistic outlook.

Schweitzer doesn't talk about religion much, unless asked. This private part of his life and upbringing doesn't appear to have much overt and obvious influence in his political life. But it's there, deeply ingrained, going back generations. "It's just difficult to separate your religious upbringing from the way you view every part of what you do on a daily basis when you get into a position like this," Schweitzer said.

For the Schweitzers the message was one of social justice. They tried to follow the model of Jesus in the Gospels, attending to the poor, sick, and downtrodden. "In Catholicism, from a very early age, that's drummed into you," Schweitzer said. "It ends up touching your heart whenever there's a decision to be made."

This ethic resonates strongly in Schweitzer's life: "I'm always thinking. I like growing business; that's exciting. I like developing energy.

... But how does it affect the last and the least? What can we do to make it better for those people who probably never will get to the front of the line? How can we make their lives better? How can we pull them along? How can we make them the most they can be? How can we make them build their self-esteem and self-respect? What more can we do?"

When it came time for high school, Mike and Brian were both looking to leave home. The high school in Geyser was small, and both youngsters wanted to follow their older brother's example. Warren had gone off to a Catholic high school in North Dakota and then enrolled in a seminary to become a priest. Neither Mike nor Brian was looking to become a priest, but they both longed for boarding school.

Adam and Kay told Mike he could go if he earned a scholarship.

So Mike pored over magazines looking for opportunities and applied for scholarships to several Catholic high schools. Finally, Holy Cross Abbey in Cañon City, Colorado, gave him a call. Mike's trip to Cañon City was only the second time he'd ever been out of Montana. The scholarship he earned gave him a chance to work for his education. And so he did janitorial work and manned the campus's switchboards. He was up well before dawn and worked weekends. Then Brian joined Mike after attending the high school in Geyser his freshman year. Like his brother, Brian had to work at the school for his scholarship.

The abbey was run by Benedictine monks and was focused on agrarian life. They ran a self-sufficient farm, which helped feed the students. And though the school was excited to enroll a farm kid, Mike wanted little to do with the farming aspect of the abbey. "I declined [to get involved with the farming]," Mike said. "I told them I'd rather do something else." So he played sports and worked and studied.

Both Brian and Mike were good students in Geyser without really trying all that hard. But it was different at the abbey. "When I got there I found out there were other smart kids as well, and they actually studied," Mike said. "It was very challenging."

The abbey was rigorous in its rules. Life was governed by bells: bells to wake you up, bells to tell you when to eat, bells to tell you when to sleep. If you missed those bells, your punishment was swift and clear. "If any of these infractions occurred, it was bend over, [and] grab your ankles," Mike said.

Students wore suits and ties and were expected to study and succeed. However, even though school was infused with the religion of the abbey, students were also encouraged to think for themselves. "The brothers, priests, and monks were devoted to education for education's sake," Mike said. "They didn't just teach; it was their life. They tried to make us learn how to think. Education is not about learning facts; education is about learning how to learn and how to think and how to question. On the one hand, it was strict. On the other hand, they gave us the freedom to think and question. In fact, it was almost demanded from us."

The boarding school also fostered close friendships. Mike and Brian were used to living a life surrounded by family. In Geyser you learned to care for people and lean on them when you got in trouble. It was the same way at the abbey, Mike said. "You developed close relationships with people. . . . Some of my best friends are from high school."

10

The New Democrats

The 2006 election was a nail-biter. In Montana Jon Tester defeated Conrad Burns by fewer than three thousand votes. In Virginia Democrat Jim Webb got the best of incumbent Republican George Allen by about seven thousand votes. Webb's race was the final one tallied and gave the Democrats a fifty-one-to-forty-nine control in the Senate. In large part a narrow referendum against the war in Iraq, the election saw Democrats pick up thirty-two seats in the House and seven seats in the Senate and control of both. In the Rocky Mountain West, states that were previously considered conservative elected Democratic governors. In the region's Senate races, however, Burns was the only incumbent to lose. Republican senators kept their seats in Wyoming, Utah, Nevada, and Arizona. In governor races Democrat Bill Ritter's win in Colorado made a solid blue streak from Montana to New Mexico. Democratic incumbent governors won in Wyoming, Arizona, and New Mexico. However, in House races, some key states and districts remained in GOP control, although significant wins by Democrats in Colorado, New Mexico, and Arizona helped turn the tide nationally.

This shift was predictable, says Jon Cowan, head of the progressive political think tank Third Way. "A lot of the new and fresh thinking, both out of a sense of vision and political necessity, has come from Rocky Mountain Democrats."

In Colorado, where Democrats retook the state at every level, they redefined the political debate away from the more traditional liberal platform held by the largely urban Democrats who dominate the coasts. "That new center is fiscally responsible and socially forward looking or modern," Cowan said. These new Democrats support gun ownership under the Second Amendment but would support reasonable gun-safety measures. They are pro-choice on abortion but would really like to see fewer of them. They promote education, health care, and renewable energy to end the country's dependence on foreign oil, he said. In a word, they are "moderate."

In a way it could be argued that being populist means being pragmatic. Schweitzer didn't jettison his own views to run as a Democrat. He held on to his fiscal conservativeness, pledged to cut taxes, and touted gun ownership. He also continues to push for alternative energy solutions and championed enhanced school funding and restructuring the state corrections system to address recidivism rates and inmate drug and mental health problems.

In a *New York Times* piece by Mark Sundeen, Markos Moulitsas Zuniga, founder of Daily Kos, is quoted as saying: "Schweitzer is the antithesis of the Democrat stereotype. Too many Democrats look like targets for the school bully. Schweitzer is a tough guy. And people like guys who will bar-fight their way across a state."

Over the past two decades, Republicans have portrayed Democrats as increasingly liberal, soft on national security, sympathetic to environmentalists, against natural resource development, and silent or liberal on important social issues such as gay marriage, religion, and abortion. Until 2006 Republicans have certainly been more adept at controlling the debate, at casting the issues in a personally flattering light. Ask your average Montanan what John Kerry stood for in the 2004 presidential campaign and you will likely hear something about taking away guns, promoting gay marriage, and locking up forests from timber harvesting. These impressions might not be accurate, but they show that the distance between the traditional Democrats and voters in the Rocky Mountain West is an ever-growing gap.

The way Cowan sees it, the Rocky Mountain Democrats are successful because they've shed the national platform and redefined themselves according to issues important to the voters in their region. By doing this, they've begun to change the tenor of the national debate. "They're trying to invent a new Democratic politics that's born out of the West," Cowan said. "The battle for the heart and soul of the Democratic Party to create a new set of ideas that work in the twenty-first century is absolutely raging."

According to Cowan this debate will bring the party a greater ability to establish and sustain a nationwide majority, but that majority won't be liberal. It will be moderate and will be more like what Democrats are seeing in the Rocky Mountains than what they've seen in the urban areas of the country.

The Conservative Right has gone too far right, removing itself from the mainstream, Cowan said. Starting with Reagan, the gap between the haves and have-nots has grown. The middle class has become endangered in a real and tangible way.

In a January 2007 article in the *New York Times Magazine,* Kurt Andersen wrote, "In 1970, a family in any given year had a one-in-fourteen chance of its income dropping by half; today, the chance is one in six. No wonder mortgage foreclosures and personal bankruptcies have quintupled during the same period. Middle-class Americans live more and more with the kind of gnawing existential uncertainty that used to be mainly a problem of the poor." To further drive home the point, in August 2007 the liberal nonprofit group United for a Fair Economy reported that CEOs of large U.S. companies made salaries 364 times greater than the average worker.

Middle-class families want someone who understands they have to work two jobs to raise a family while still trying to find some money to put aside in a retirement plan. And someday, if they're lucky, they would like to give their children money for college and maybe even a down payment on their first home. At a Democratic rally in D.C. in 2006, Schweitzer said, "Democrats will win elections when they figure out how to talk to those families."

These families don't want the government intruding in their lives, but they want good roads, good schools, social security, and health care. They don't mind paying taxes if the taxes are fair. They don't often think about the environment, but when they do, they think about how it would be nice to make it cleaner. They want the price of gas to go down and wouldn't mind buying an affordable hybrid car. They go to church but don't want people telling them what to believe. They get uncomfortable talking about abortion and gay marriage, and though they're important issues, they sure are tired of people arguing about them. They want the basic liberties of free speech and gun ownership, even if they don't hunt or carry a gun.

"People in Washington get this absurd view that the typical Western voter is someone who's living on their own piece of land and hates everything about the government and that's just wrong," Cowan said.

Elaine Kamarck, professor at the Kennedy School of Government at Harvard and a policy advisor for Al Gore's presidential campaign in 2000, also feels the Democratic Party is starting to look West. Kamarck worked in the Clinton White House and is credited for helping found the New Democrat movement in the 1980s that helped elect Clinton. Kamarck, like Cowan, sees the Democratic Party changing focus again. "There's a kind of an emerging philosophy that the Rocky Mountain states may come out of their 'off the radar screen' category when it comes to presidential politics," she said.

In both presidential elections, 2000 and 2004, the tightness of the races forced the players to look toward rural America. Even Montana, with only three electoral votes, drew attention. And the Rocky Mountain states, taken as a whole, could potentially swing the outcome of a tight election. "Small states now often get contested because of an electoral-vote scenario that's evenly split," Kamarck said. "Suddenly they've become big players in presidential elections."

But succeeding in the West will mean that the Democrats will have to not only address issues of national importance — Iraq, immigration, health care — but face the regional concerns as well: population growth, agriculture, water issues, natural resource and wildlife management, and so on.

Kamarck maintains that the Democratic Party has become more centrist since Clinton, but the Republican Party has continued to push right and is losing voters. And Cowan agrees. They've continued to push the either-or philosophy that many people can't identify with, he said. "The majority of voters in the U.S., and this is particularly true for places out West, they're really sick and tired of either-or politics." The idea that you're either pro-choice or pro-life, prowar or proterrorist, proguns or pro–gun control, just doesn't resonate with the majority. "People sense that that's just a bankrupt approach to politics," he said. "It's a dishonest approach to politics."

"The politicians who best articulate a principle politics that transcend an either-or setup — those will be the people that lead the Democratic Party to modernize."

11

The Old Democrats

"The idea is that there's this trait of individualism in Montana," Bob Brown said. Former Montana legislator and secretary of state, the man who lost to Schweitzer in 2004 is a professorial figure. Balding with round glasses, he favors a dress shirt but no tie, just a sport coat and blue jeans. He's now a senior fellow at the O'Connor Center for the Rocky Mountain West, a regional think tank. He also teaches history at the University of Montana, a position which seems to suit him. Turns out, he has an almost encyclopedic knowledge of Montana's past.

I sat down with Brown in the spring of 2007. I've known him since he was secretary of state and always liked him. Now I was interested in hearing his thoughts on Schweitzer's role in Montana's history, and this was fine with Brown, although he didn't care to talk about Schweitzer's performance as a governor. The race was in the past, and he didn't want to go back to it or criticize his old adversary.

In discussing Montana's historically conspicuous thread of individualism, Brown talks about the "reasonable and prudent" speed limit in place from 1995 to 1999. You could drive as fast as the law felt was safe. It was also still legal to drink and drive until 2005, as long as you weren't intoxicated. Now it's illegal, but the fine is $100 and the violation doesn't go on your driving record. Out here, environmentalists are people who still hunt and fish. They may chain themselves to a tree to keep loggers from cutting it down, but check their freezer and you'll find steaks from last year's deer.

"This independent streak sets us aside somewhat," Brown said.

While voters in Montana don't register under party affiliation, recent polls have Montana divided fairly evenly among Republican, Democrat, and Independent. In 1992 Ross Perot had more than 26 percent of the vote in Montana while Clinton won the state with 37 percent. Max Baucus has served in the U.S. Senate for nearly thirty years. In the 110th Congress he voted with his party about 88 percent of the time. Only six other Democratic senators broke away from their party more often.

Bob Brown describes how, during the Civil War, politics across the nation looked very different. The South was staunchly Democrat while the Northeast was firmly Republican. In Montana during the 1860s, many of the immigrant miners were from Southern states, who had, thanks to the Civil War, brought with them a fierce dislike for Republicans. Early settlers to the state also tended to be independent-minded Democrats. These first settlers set an early tone for Montana's politics, Brown said: "The Democrats have had a greater dominance as a party than the Republicans have."

However, Republicans' recent dominance was fairly complete. The three governors before Schweitzer were Republicans and though the state legislature shifted a little between Democratic and Republican control, the Montana of the 1990s was clearly red. This could have been a reflection of national political trends, as the national Republican Party was gaining strength.

But in the scope of history, the Montana Republican success in the 1990s was somewhat of an aberration, Brown said. In the 1880s, as gold segued to copper, the huge mines in Butte became the state's political and economic power. These mines were controlled by William A. Clark and Marcus Daly, both Democrats. Homesteaders in eastern Montana came from a wide variety of ethnic backgrounds—Norwegian, German, Irish—but most were also Democrats. Montana's cattle boom in the 1870s to 1890s was fueled, in large part, by Texas Democrats. In fact it was Montana's Democratic leanings that kept it from becoming a state. When Montana was finally voted into the Union in 1889, it had been a territory longer than any other state—twenty-five years. The Republican-controlled Congress in the post–Civil War years wasn't anxious to bring in another Democratic state.

In fact, the ultraconservative and controversial Conrad Burns, unseated by Jon Tester in 2006, is the only Republican senator ever to be reelected in Montana's history. He served eighteen years, from 1988 to 2006.

To confuse Montana's political history even more, both parties saw splits during the early 1900s. Progressives broke ranks and fought to pull the state out from under the powerful hand of the Amalgamated Mining Company, which came into existence when Daly sold out to Standard Oil in 1899. Later, when Clark also sold his copper mine to Amalgamated Mining, the company had a nearly complete stranglehold on politics and newspapers around Montana. Enter the socialist Industrial Workers of the World, a labor organization that pushed for fairer wages and better working conditions, among other things. Through the course of fighting "the wobblies," Clark and Daly manipulated the state's political landscape as best they could, trying to minimize governmental control over their empire.

Through all these various political contortions, from the first wave of immigrants to the Freemen making a stand outside of Jordan, the only common thread to Montana politics seems to be the unpredictable independence of the electorate. (As a side note, and interestingly, the Montana Freemen were led by Schweitzer's cousin LeRoy Schweitzer. Brian Schweitzer, however, shrugs off the connection. "I've got about two thousand relatives in Montana. I think I have fifty first cousins or more.")

If you are a politician who aspires to political office, to a governorship, how do you codify or quantify that unpredictability? How do you try to appeal to an electorate that, by definition, avoids thinking of itself as an organized body? In Schweitzer's good ol' boy persona, he's perhaps found a key. You show the people that you are one of them.

12

The Making of a Soil Scientist

Brian Schweitzer graduated from Holy Cross Abbey and, like his brother Mike (who went to Colorado College), stayed in Colorado, choosing Colorado State University in Fort Collins. Initially he wanted to be a veterinarian but soon decided that it wasn't a career that would offer him the kind of life he was looking for. "I just kind of lost interest. I still liked animals but, you know, I could see that being a veterinarian meant that you were just going to be an animal mechanic or plumber. You worked on one animal at a time. I had dreams of doing bigger things."

So he looked for something that could place him on a larger stage, give him an opportunity to make a difference on a grander scale. He liked school; he was smart and earned good grades, although classes with three hundred kids packing auditoriums didn't really appeal to him.

Things changed when he took a soil-classification class taught by a professor named Heil. "Suddenly it just clicked. I was sitting in a class, I wasn't taking a note, [and] it just clicked," Schweitzer said. "That's a guy who got me excited enough to study soils." He describes himself as an ambitious person. It is a trait in his character that has literally led him around the world. His passion for studying soils suddenly opened his mind to larger possibilities. He switched from studying animal health to international agronomy: "I wanted to go overseas. I wanted to see the world. I didn't even know what it looked like over there. Over there was just somewhere else."

Before being elected governor of Montana, Schweitzer hadn't held any public office. However, he had been through at least two elections. While Schweitzer was at Colorado State, the school reenergized an agronomy club. Other schools like Nebraska, Purdue, and Kansas State all had agronomy clubs. Every year, they sent contingents of students to the national convention. When an agronomy club at CSU was finally established, Schweitzer was one of the first members, and when the time for the national convention came around, the club members randomly picked who would represent CSU. "We drew straws. My roommate and I drew the long straws. They accused us of fixing it but we didn't. If we knew how to, we might've, but we didn't," Schweitzer said.

Like many other times in life, Schweitzer did his homework: "Before I went, I did a little research and found out they actually had national officers. CSU had never even sent anybody before. It was all kind of controlled by the old big ag universities. So I thought, ah what the hell, and I ran for office . . . and I got elected vice president of the organization."

The decision to run for the office seemed casual. But it speaks to Schweitzer's ambition for leadership. He could have attended the conference and nothing more. But that's not his way.

During the simple election, Schweitzer campaigned with the students at the convention and won. At the time the accomplishment felt impressive to him. It had a David and Goliath feel to it—the kind of battle, not incidentally, he still seems anxious to take on. But if he had political ambitions back then, he won't admit to it. However, this scenario, as much as anything in his younger years, foreshadows the politician he would become. Even as a college student, he wasn't intimidated by long odds, nor would he be satisfied with just being vice president. At the convention the following year, his senior year, Schweitzer was elected president of the association.

During his undergraduate years he also worked for the Joseph Schlitz Brewing Company, helping barley farmers develop their crops and then buying and grading their barley when they delivered it. Having grown up on a farm and ranch and (no doubt) not being opposed to drinking the occasional beer himself, he was, as it turned out, a natural.

13

Graduate School

After college Schweitzer applied to graduate schools around the country—Arizona, North Carolina, Hawaii—all schools with top programs in farming tropical soils. He focused on tropical soils because it would be a master's degree that complimented his bachelor's in international agronomy and give him the necessary education to farm in countries with warm climates. Despite several acceptances he decided to head home to Montana State University instead: "I thought, God, I love Montana, and if I'm going to pack my bags and be gone, I want to spend a couple of more years fishing and skiing before I head to the tropics."

Marie Boehm, now a research scientist with Agriculture and Agri-Food Canada in Saskatchewan, went to graduate school with Schweitzer at MSU: "Brian was quite fun because he was a larger-than-life kind of guy, even as a young student."

When Boehm and Schweitzer were attending school, many students were there on the G.I. Bill, she said. In fact, MSU had a large number of out-of-state students, which made Schweitzer a sort of anomaly. "Students like Brian from Montana were kind of a minority," Boehm said. "There were students from almost everywhere else *but* Montana."

But in this environment Schweitzer seemed to thrive. Boehm remembers him as talkative person, a fine debater, and a hard worker. Interestingly, she didn't see him as much of a scientist. "Brian went in, did something, did a good job, but didn't agonize relentlessly over the details. . . . He probably knew that he wasn't going to be an academic for the rest of his life." Boehm added, "He's not a dilly-dallier."

The day she heard Schweitzer had been elected governor of Montana, she remembered one faculty member as having said that Schweitzer would end up either in jail or as governor. She added, "You always knew he was going to achieve something, one way or another."

Larry Munn, now a professor of soil science at the University of Wyoming, was an assistant professor working on his doctorate at MSU when Schweitzer was there. Like Marie he remembers him as an outgoing, jovial guy who was as interested in social events as in school: "Brian was always an extremely outgoing person, and he either had a tremendous amount of self-confidence or he made himself look that way." Munn has been teaching students for more than twenty-five years, and Schweitzer still stands out from the bunch.

Schweitzer was a debater, Munn said. It wasn't that he liked to argue; it was more civilized. He just liked to banter back and forth about ideas and philosophies. He was also people oriented. He remembered names of students and other people around campus and always knew what was going on at the school. And all the stories he told seemed to center around his experiences with others.

During graduate school Schweitzer lived on his stipend as a teacher's assistant, about $300 a month. He remembered one old house where he and his roommates only heated the living room. That way they could leave the food out in the kitchen where it wouldn't spoil. "I did a lot of my research down at Little John's," he said. "That was the country-and-western hangout."

As Schweitzer began his thesis, he started looking for a job. It didn't take long for him to catch a break. Food Development Corporation, a company working large tracts of land around the West, had landed a contract to set up farming in Libya and offered him an agronomy position there, south of Tripoli. They would need him within a couple of months.

But Schweitzer still had a thesis to finish. He told his advisor, professor Jerry Nielson, that he was going to have to finish while he was in Libya. But Nielson knew from experience that it was unlikely the thesis would be done once Schweitzer was working outside the country with other things on his mind, so he promised to help Schweitzer push his thesis through before he left. They got it done, and Schweitzer was soon off to the Middle East.

14

Accessible but Guarded

Like his predecessors Brian Schweitzer maintains an open-door policy. Particularly in this post-9/11 age of increased homeland security, it's surprising and somewhat disconcerting that you can park behind the Capitol building in Helena, nod at the bored security guard, walk past the life-size statue of Jeannette Rankin, and just stroll into Schweitzer's office. "Is Brian available?" But as it turns out, Montanans have always been able to shake hands with their elected officials.

When I first moved to Montana from Oregon in 1998, I'd never met a politician until I went to a prayer breakfast hosted by Governor Marc Racicot. I stood in the greeting line, surprised by how short he was, as well as by the strength of his handshake. He commented on my tie, and I asked him about his. By the time his successor, Judy Martz, left office, she and I were friends. When Schweitzer returns my call, he starts out by saying, "Hey, this is Brian."

It's important to keep perspective. Journalists and politicians tend to maintain a cautious and courteous kind of mutual symbiosis. Politicians need journalists to help communicate with their constituencies. Journalists need access to politicians for the interviews. But this is Montana, too—one of the few places in America where the very rich shop at the same IGAs as the very poor. People are still people.

With Brian Schweitzer, however—and as I would learn through the course of writing this book—the obstacles involved in getting to know him have little to do with ease of access. I've seen Schweitzer take a knee to talk to Millie Kieffer, a ninety-three-year-old ranch woman who was telling Schweitzer about a ditch that flows across her land. I heard him tell stories about drinking whiskey to Milt Datsopoulos, a prominent defense attorney, at Stockman's Bar in Missoula. I heard him stump for Jon Tester, Democratic U.S. senator from Big Sandy, on the *Ed Schultz Show*. He told Schultz that Tester "had a belly the size of a grain bin," but that he'd beat Conrad Burns to be the next senator for Montana. He cusses about politics, swigs beer at bars, and whoops like Howard Dean at Democratic rallies.

I asked Schweitzer once about how he had developed as a politician, and he began talking about the potential for energy in Montana. He deflects questions without any sort of skill, just stubbornness. He's living the adage, "They can't print what you don't say."

Politicians are held to a different standard than those in the private sector. Rightly or wrongly, we expect them to be cleaner, less sullied by the baser human impulses. Oddly enough, however, the media consistently focuses on what politicians say and do in the public eye, with the exception of scandals in their private life. For a politician inclined toward privacy in his or her home life, a certain type of reticence can be surprisingly easy to achieve.

Brian Schweitzer's grandparents homesteaded in Montana. This is their original house, located thirty miles north of Gilford. COURTESY SCHWEITZER FAMILY

A studio photo taken in 1973, upon Schweitzer's high school graduation.

COURTESY SCHWEITZER FAMILY

Nancy Hupp met Brian Schweitzer at Montana State University. She was studying botany and he was a graduate assistant in one of her classes. This image was taken shortly before they were married in 1982.

COURTESY SCHWEITZER FAMILY

Nancy Hupp and Brian Schweitzer were married on January 23, 1982. All of Brian's immediate family were present including, standing from left, his sister Mary, his brother Walter, his sister-in-law Ingela, Ingela's husband Warren, Nancy and Brian, Brian's mother Kay and father Adam, his then-sister-in-law Kim and, kneeling to the right, Kim's then-husband Mike Schweitzer. Kneeling to the left is Darwin Schweitzer. COURTESY SCHWEITZER FAMILY

The future governor of Montana began his career working as an agronomist in Libya and Saudi Arabia. Shown here are three bedouins in Saudi Arabia's Wadi al-Radir. The governor explains that they were just "out fooling with guns. They're like us, they like to go out and target practice."
COURTESY SCHWEITZER FAMILY

This group of bedouins was photographed next to a pivot sprinkler near Al Khanj. During his time in the Middle East, Schweitzer acted as consultant on various irrigation projects. COURTESY SCHWEITZER FAMILY

This 1985 photo of "Nasser," the business manager for the Saleh Rajhi family—owners of the farm on which Schweitzer worked—was taken in Saudi Arabia's Wadi Dawassir, or Dawassir Valley.

COURTESY SCHWEITZER FAMILY

During his first run for office (against Republican U.S. Senator Conrad Burns) Schweitzer emphasized the need for prescription drug care reform—an issue that resonated with older voters. COURTESY J.O.B.S.

A family Christmas in Whitefish,
Montana, 2003. Brian and Nancy's
three children are, from left to right,
Ben, Khai, and Katrina.
COURTESY SCHWEITZER FAMILY

Schweitzer swathing mint on
his property outside of Whitefish.
COURTESY SCHWEITZER FAMILY

*At the world-famous Crow Fair in Crow Agency, Montana, Schweitzer tried his
hand at riding a green broke horse.* COURTESY J.O.B.S.

A hunter and fisherman, Brian Schweitzer has found political success in part by emphasizing his love of guns and sport.
COURTESY J.O.B.S.

Schweitzer campaigns with his future lieutenant governor John Bohlinger.
COURTESY J.O.B.S.

Appearing for a fund-raiser on behalf of Saint Vincent's Hospital, from left to right, Lieutenant Governor John Bohlinger, his late wife Bette, and Nancy and Brian Schweitzer COURTESY J.O.B.S.

15

The Governor's Office

Montana's capital city, Helena, is a town of about twenty-six thousand souls, most of them unaffiliated with government. And yet there's an undercurrent of quiet pride at the role the city plays in the state's leadership, in the decisions that are being made, even now, just around the corner from where we might be having lunch.

The Capitol itself—sandstone and granite with a slate gray dome—stands overlooking the town, visible from all directions. It's a majestic building with high ceilings decorated with murals painted by Charles A. Pedretti, depicting scenes from Montana's past: mining, ranching, exploring. In front of the Capitol is a bronze statue of Thomas Francis Meagher mounted on a horse, saber held over his head. Cowboy artist Charles M. Russell contributed a twelve-by-twenty-five-foot mural, *Lewis and Clark Meeting the Flathead Indians*, to the house chambers. Edgar Paxson's paintings decorate the lobby outside the house chambers and bronze statues of the late Mike and Maureen Mansfield welcome visitors as they climb the marble staircase to the second floor. Next to the Mansfields stands a dignified statue of Montana's most famous female politician, Jeannette Rankin, the first woman to serve in the U.S. Congress and the only dissenting vote against World War II.

A mile or so away from the Capitol, a popular steak house displays photos of every Montana governor since statehood in 1889, bookended by Democrats Joseph Kemp Toole and Brian Schweitzer. Toole had served as Montana's territorial delegate to Congress for four years before being elected as the state's first governor. An attorney, he went back to his law practice in Helena after his first term and then was reelected in 1901 and 1905. It was Toole who largely presented Montana's case for statehood to Congress, and his statesmanship in D.C. helped him win his first election. His first term as governor was noted for its role in the development and ratification of the state's constitution, as well as for instituting laws governing elections. He also promoted a progressive agenda, including signing laws related to the establishment of an eight-hour workday, school funding, mine safety, and rudimentary environmental protection. John Morrison and Catherine Wright Morrison, in their book *Mavericks: The Lives and Battles of Montana's Political Legends,* wrote, "With skill, devotion, and courage, Joe Toole launched and captained Montana on its maiden voyage and thereby distinguished himself as the father of the Treasure State."

Another significant governor from Montana's past, and one that Schweitzer has studied and reveres, is Republican Joseph Dixon. Born in 1867 in North Carolina, Dixon came to Missoula in 1891, working his way up through local and state politics to become a U.S. congressman and senator. During his political career he owned controlling interest in the *Missoulian,* which proved advantageous during his various campaigns for office.

Dixon's rise in politics was tied to another Republican, Theodore Roosevelt. Dixon ran Roosevelt's unsuccessful presidential reelection campaign in 1912, and, in the wake of the defeat (Roosevelt lost the primary to Howard Taft), Roosevelt and Dixon formed a third party, the Progressive Bull Moose Party. Dixon was elected the national chairman, and Roosevelt was nominated as its presidential candidate. The two men came to Montana to preside over the state Bull Moose convention. According to the Morrisons, the convention ratified the national Progressive platform, as well as adopted "its own platform calling for . . . public guarantee of bank deposits, equal suffrage for women, public grain inspection, graduated income and inheritance tax laws, arbitration of labor disputes, prohibition of child labor, an employers' liability (workers' compensation) act, investment of state funds in farm mortgages, sanitary laws for mines and mills, a short-form ballot law, and 'pure seed' law, support of widows and orphans of convicts, reorganization of state educational institutions, and a full railroad crew law, among other measures." These were issues popular with Montana, and Dixon was perceived as the leader.

To understand Dixon's success and failures, it's important to first look at copper mining in Montana. Amalgamated Copper, or "The Company," began in 1899 when Standard Oil bought Marcus Daly's Anaconda Copper Mine. And while big eastern money was behind it (including Henry H. Rogers, William Rockefeller, James Stillman, and A. C. Burrage), its center was in Butte. These men routinely paid off politicians on both sides of the aisle and owned all but one major newspaper. "Opposition," the Morrisons wrote, "was not tolerated. When dissenters spoke out, Anaconda [the company] would tighten its grip, crushing its antagonists and sometimes strangling the community. The company made itself the enemy of the people and engendered a public hatred that defined the face of Montana's politics for decades." To quell strikes, the company would lay off miners and close mines. In its newspapers, through editorials and biased (often fictitious) articles, it drew a bead on any public figure who dared oppose its agendas. The Progressive Era in Montana was a direct response to the Amalgamated Copper's influence.

Dixon ran for and was elected governor in 1920. Faced with a $2 million deficit, in his first speech to the legislative session, he proposed a suite of tax-reform measures including establishing an income tax, inheritance tax, and a tax on public services and industrial corporations.

"Startling enough for Montana in the year 1920, but there was more," wrote K. Ross Toole in his book *Twentieth Century Montana: A State of Extremes.* "He [Dixon] advocated a three percent gross tax on oil. Montana dry farming sections, he said, 'are now literally staggering, at a time of severe depression . . . under heavy taxation.' Yet Montana coal mines in the year 1919, mines owned largely by the Northern Pacific Railroad, produced in excess of 3,000,000 tons of coal. They showed little taxable 'net proceeds,' yet in fact they had made $7,757,103 gross, paying tax on *net* proceeds of $682." Toole goes on to point out that "the Anaconda Company had paid no tax at all on proceeds." In 1922 Amalgamated Copper had earned more than $20 million off of its metal mines but paid only $13,559 in taxes.

The speech heralded a dark time for Dixon in Helena. Amalgamated Copper pounded him in the press for four years. His initiatives never got off the ground and the citizens never had a good chance to hear his thoughts because the company dominated the media. Dixon ran for reelection in 1924 but was defeated by John E. Erickson.

However, while the company was busy bludgeoning Dixon, it missed an initiative he had placed on the ballot that taxed the mines' proceeds and started drawing money into state coffers from the immense wealth in Butte. In part due to his opposition to the company, Dixon is now considered by historians as one of Montana's greatest governors.

Dixon is the Montana governor Schweitzer relates to the most. He points to the fact that Dixon wasn't afraid to stand up to the corrupt influences that permeated state government in his time. Dixon didn't back down, and in the end it cost him a second term as governor.

Connected with Dixon, in history and in Schweitzer's mind, is Theodore Roosevelt. Roosevelt and Dixon were aligned politically in the national progressive movement. Roosevelt was elected president as a Republican, but stood up to big business corruption in government and championed the conservation movement — things that were not typical of Republicans at the time, Schweitzer said. "Those are the kind of people I respect. The ones who will stand up in their own party and say to their own folks 'I love you to death, but you're wrong on this.'"

The last Democratic governor prior to Schweitzer was Ted Schwinden. Responsible for establishing Montana's Department of Commerce, which promoted both the "Made in Montana" program as well as Travel Montana, Schwinden was apparently a rare combination of charisma and humility. Coming into office in 1980 with a struggling Montana economy, he pushed through a bed tax and promoted a fiscal conservativism that appealed to both sides of the aisle. He was partisan and believed in Democratic ideals, but that didn't keep him from working with Republicans or appointing qualified people outside the party. The director of the Department of Commerce under Schwinden, Gary Buchanan, still has enormous respect for him. Buchanan was thirty-one when Schwinden appointed him, but that didn't stop the governor from giving him a lot of responsibility and providing him room to grow in his job. "He was by far the best boss I've ever had," Buchanan said.

When Schwinden's second term ended, Montana started on a sixteen-year stint of three Republican governors — Stan Stephens, Marc Racicot and Judy Martz, the most popular being Marc Racicot. Racicot was born in Libby, Montana. He served as state attorney general for eight years before winning the governorship in 1992. According to journalist Chuck Johnson, Racicot felt government should be small and efficient. He inherited a $200 million deficit and in response cut the budget by $99 million and raised taxes by $99 million. The bold move worked, and Racicot enjoyed a fairly smooth two terms. In fact, he was, at times, Montana's most popular governor ever, with approval ratings peaking at 83 percent. When he left office in 2000, it was with approval ratings of more than 70 percent.

The black spot on Racicot's tenure came in the form of utility deregulation. Racicot and many of the other Republican leaders in the state felt that allowing energy rates to be determined by the open market would give Montanans better deals. It didn't work. Once deregulation occurred, Montana Power, the state's main service provider, sold its electric production to PPL, a Pennsylvania company, who under deregulation could then sell to the highest bidder. The result is that Montana citizens and businesses pay much more now for power.

In an interview with Johnson in 2000, Racicot reflected on his years as governor. He was pleased with the restructuring of the state's workers' compensation system that was accomplished under his watch. He was also happy with the investments made into the state's infrastructure, hospitals, and schools. "As he has in the past, Racicot doesn't take personal credit for achievements during his tenure, saying the executive and legislative branches worked together and often with local officials to accomplish them. Racicot believes he helped, 'by disciplining our discourse,' [to] create the right atmosphere in which people could get good things done," wrote Johnson.

Racicot's lieutenant governor, Judy Martz, followed her mentor into office. As awkward with the press as Racicot was adept, her approval ratings quickly went south. She was plagued by small scandals writ large, the most tragic being a drunk-driving incident that involved her closest advisor, Shane Hedges. Republican house majority leader Paul Sliter was killed in the accident, and Hedges resigned from Martz's staff, pleading guilty to negligent homicide. He served six months in a prerelease center. The night of the accident, Martz washed Hedges's bloody clothes. Controversy immediately swirled as to whether or not she had tampered with evidence. Martz was later absolved of wrongdoing.

Then there was a land deal gone sour. Martz bought property from a company that bordered land her family owned near Butte. The price paid was reportedly lower than market value. The Montana Democratic Party filed an ethics complaint against Martz, but the Montana commissioner of political practices found no wrongdoing. She left office after one term with the percentage of Montanans who approved of her job hovering around 25 percent. While her popularity ratings were bleak, I found her to be a kind woman and well intentioned, although one who was never entirely comfortable with the spotlight that came with her office.

Though many saw her as a poor governor, she provided Montanans something unique in politics: a frank and straight-talking leader. Chuck Johnson wrote, "She is a strong-willed person with strong opinions . . . Like most people from Butte, she always said what was on her mind. Reporters liked that." Regardless, she often claimed she was getting a "hard shake" from Montana's media. At one point she even refused interviews with two capital reporters. However, Martz came into office faced with a deficit and a depressed economy and, through tax cuts and a focus on the economic development, left her successor, Schweitzer, with a nearly $300 million surplus.

And now there's Brian Schweitzer, a governor who seems to value, above all else, the notion of legitimacy. "People don't have to agree with all of the issues you take up," he told Charlie Rose. "They just want to know that you believe it, that you will do the right thing, that you are not a phony."

16

Libya, Etc.

Even taking into account Schweitzer's energetic personality, his professor Larry Munn said it was still a shock when he announced that he was headed to the Sahara to grow wheat for Muammar al-Qaddafi. "It was very unique for Brian to take off like he did."

In Libya, Food Development Corporation was taking on a massive project—farming the desert. In 1980 Qaddafi had been dictator for more than a decade. Given his strained relationships with the West, he feared that Libya was too dependent on foreign food and that this dependence could cost them greatly if international sanctions were instituted against the country. He contracted with FDC to develop a farm in the Sahara, five hundred miles south of Tripoli. The contract was for five years, after which FDC would hand the farm over to the Libyan government.

Henry Kartchner, who started FDC, took up the contract and began hiring. His company eventually developed farms and agriculture projects throughout the Middle East. And while Kartchner hasn't paid attention to Schweitzer's political career (he wasn't even aware that Schweitzer had been elected governor of Montana), his company now has a sister venture, Fuel Development Company, which is developing small biodiesel plants in Texas—a venture right up Schweitzer's alley.

At the time of the Libyan project, FDC had major farming projects in America. But developing farms in the Middle East was a new venture. No one was really doing it at that time. Along with the agricultural startup, the contract stated FDC had to train Libyans to farm, as well as send one hundred Libyans to college in America to learn agriculture.

The obvious problem with farming in the desert is water. To overcome that, FDC drilled wells a thousand feet deep and installed center pivot sprinklers. The undertaking was enormous. At one time FDC had about six hundred men on the project. "When you went in the desert, there wasn't anything there so it was like an invasion," Kartchner said. "We had to ship over everything from toothpicks to D8 caterpillars."

And the environment was hostile. Temperatures would climb to more than 130 degrees in the summer and drop below freezing in the winter. "Sometimes the wind would blow a whole field away," Schweitzer recalled. "Forty acres would just move, become a dune a half mile away." But they could grow crops year around, corn or sorghum in the summer and wheat in the winter. "To farm the desert is completely different than trying to farm normally," Kartchner said.

"My job was to build and maintain the lab where we did soil and plant tissue testing," Schweitzer said. "We did it all on the farm. I trained people to work in the lab and then designed the irrigation scheduling and fertility scheduling and pesticide management." There was little precedent for the work he was doing—the area had no log of weather data to assist in the schedules for sowing or irrigation—so it was like starting with a blank slate.

Other countries sent in companies to farm the region, but they struggled. "Some of the foreign companies had a hell of a time," Kartchner said. "We were really the only American company in there and we were of course the best." Despite the challenges the crop yields were good.

"If you can get water to it, the desert is actually a fertile place to farm," Schweitzer said.

Kartchner remembered Schweitzer as one of his first hires on the project. Schweitzer's starting salary was $2,000 a month. "I figured that was a pretty good wage, considering I was only making $300 a month in grad school," Schweitzer said. The men at the farm worked ninety days in country (seven days a week) followed by thirty days at home. The company provided housing, food, and entertainment, usually in the form of movies. They wouldn't allow women or alcohol. Kartchner had a hard time holding on to men for more than a year: "But that was normal. The Americans really don't like to be over where there's no women, whiskey, or song."

But they were pioneers, which appealed to Schweitzer. He was on land that no one had farmed, in a country that was in a constant state of political and military turmoil. He was seeing the world, by God. He was helping lead a monumental farming project in, of all places, the Sahara, and he wasn't even twenty-five years old.

This first tour in the Middle East was a benchmark for Schweitzer. He had set out with a goal and he had succeeded. He was making his mark. "I relish the opportunity wherever it is, whatever I'm doing, to try something that no one ever has—to try and climb a mountain that nobody thought you could. I don't have a fear of failure. If I try something and give it my best and it doesn't work, then I say, 'Well, I learned something from that.' Some folks aren't wired that way. I'm willing to go in and try something that nobody else would."

17

The Middle East Again

During his stint with FDC, Schweitzer saw a job opening with a Swedish engineering company in the process of constructing, in Saudi Arabia, the world's largest dairy farm. He contacted the company, Alfa Laval, and while he was home on a break from Libya, they sent someone to interview him. That preliminary meeting led to an interview in New York and, ultimately, another farming job in the Middle East. Schweitzer would be in charge of developing the irrigation system for a dairy farm, a step up. "When I went to the project in Saudi Arabia, I was effectively in charge of all things that had to do with irrigation and crops," he said.

But since he was the only American, he had to learn how to communicate in many different languages. The manager meetings at the farm were mostly held in Swedish, so he learned enough of the language to get by. The farm also employed workers Schweitzer referred to as "Third World nationals." They came from all over the world—Thailand, Pakistan, the Philippines, Egypt, and the Sudan. So, Schweitzer said, he learned enough of those languages to communicate.

At this project, more than the Libya farm, Schweitzer was under the microscope. His normal jovial nature was put away and his more serious, more intense personality emerged. "My nature is I'm quick to wit, I'm quick to laugh—quick to tell a story, quick to tell a story on myself, quick to tell a story on one of my coworkers," he said. "But [in Saudia Arabia] I had to be serious as a heart attack."

Schweitzer was the youngest man on the project and the only American. He was also making more money than many of his peers— $3,500 a month at the beginning of the project and $4,500 a month when he left nearly three years later. "Being the youngest and being the only American, I had to prove myself from day one. In order to have people respect you in the workplace who are older than you and of a different nationality—I had to be serious."

Schweitzer also points to his innate ability to work hard. "What I did to prove myself—if you were to ask somebody today who was the hardest worker, who showed up first, who worked the longest hours, who was—when he was off the job—was still doing work in his head and with a calculator? Everybody, hands down, would say that would be that guy Brian Schweitzer. Nobody cold keep up with him. He was the hardest worker. Now, the reason I could do that was I liked it. I was doing what I loved and I loved what I was doing." Much as with the Libyan project, Schweitzer was starting from scratch. "We went into a raw piece of desert and drilled wells and started planting crops, building corrals for the cattle and the dairy processing facilities. . . . We had water treatment plants; we generated our own electricity. We were completely self-sufficient." Since many Saudis are lactose intolerant, Schweitzer said, the milk was processed into a yogurt-type liquid. Then the farm shipped the product all over the kingdom.

After nearly three years the dairy farm was up and running. All that was left was farm management, which, although a big job, didn't appeal to Schweitzer. With two successful large farming projects behind him, he now had the resume to strike out on his own. He started a private farm-consulting business in cooperation with a Saudi partner (foreigners weren't allowed to own their own businesses in Saudi Arabia, not without a sponsor). Schweitzer would set up farms and give a share of the profits to his partner. Schweitzer said, "I effectively ran it as if it was my own company."

The farms he started were large operations, ten to thirty thousand acres of irrigated land, growing mostly wheat and alfalfa but sometimes vegetables as well. "We'd go out and mobilize in the desert and drill a hundred wells and build a hundred center pivots and build all the housing and build all the grain storage and build all the roads and install the generators and water treatment systems, and we'd have instant farms," he said. "We'd go from a desert to an irrigated farm in six months."

At that time the Saudi government was heavily subsidizing farms, Schweitzer said. If a family had land they wanted to put into production, and if it fared well in a feasibility study, the government would essentially pay to build the farm and then buy the wheat back for about $32 a bushel, ten times what it brought in America.

"Anybody who wanted to build a farm, their first choice was to somehow get me involved in it because I had been successful," Schweitzer said proudly. "I was in pretty high demand. I was just a young guy, but I was the guy that had built the successful projects in Arabia."

Despite their vast cultural differences, Schweitzer saw some similarities between himself and the Saudis: "They're a people who love the land. They'd never been involved in irrigation like this, but they loved the land."

The people he typically worked with had a passion for the harvest, for seeing dry land turned into farms. Schweitzer related to this as well: "There's nothing cooler than buying a ranch. There's nothing cooler than adding to that ranch. There's nothing cooler than making that ranch better."

The Saudis evolved from a nomadic culture, Schweitzer said. In fact, in areas of the region, people are still largely nomadic. These nomads are called bedouins. When Schweitzer made deals with families to build farms, the negotiations were very different than what occurred in Western culture.

"I ended up working for a lot of different clients, people who owned manufacturing facilities, shipyards, banks—Saudis who were business people and wanted to get into agriculture. Oftentimes the real negotiations occurred in the desert. They're children of bedouins and they were most comfortable in the desert. So, if you really wanted to negotiate business you had to go to the desert with them."

So Schweitzer would follow his potential clients, some of whom were sheikhs (an Arab leader) or princes, to the desert. "They'd drive fifty, eighty, a hundred miles out into the desert—off of any road and they'd have a bunch of their people, servants, set up these big tents and lay out beautiful carpets right down on the sand. They'd bring a truck load of sheep and goats to eat for the weekend."

Once they got settled, the dialogue would begin. However, in the bedouin culture, it was a sign of weakness to bring up the business dealing at hand. "You learn, culturally, it's a standoff. The first one to bring up actual business was going to lose." Instead, Schweitzer's hosts would give him things to eat and drink while the weekend wore on and tales were told. "You'd talk about the old days, what it was like to live in the desert, camel racing, their favorite camels. They'd talk about their wives, the oldest one, the youngest one, they'd talk about their kids, they'd talk about vacation—everything but business, and remember you were there to negotiate a deal."

It was important to be patient if you wanted to make a good deal, he said. Bedouins are never open with what they want in the negotiation. Their goal is to get the other person to reveal their desires. "Knowledge is power for a bedouin," Schweitzer said. "They believe when you know what's important [to them] you'll give them that and take everything else."

In Western culture, two people enter into a negotiation and detail what their principles are—what they need and want. It's an issue of time, he said. Americans don't want to waste their days negotiating deals. Western businessmen couldn't imagine taking days, weeks or months to discuss a business transaction. So to run a successful business in the Middle East, Schweitzer had to think like a bedouin and understand how to match them in negotiations.

"You'd just wait them out. Sometimes it was hours, sometimes it was days. And it was important for you not to be the one who was the pushy one. A bedouin is the best negotiator in the world," Schweitzer said. "So I was ambivalent about everything. Whatever was important to me I never let them know, because they'd never let me know."

Negotiating the bedouin way is a skill Schweitzer uses as governor. He describes a typical political negotiation like this: "When I sit down with legislators and they say 'Oh well I want this bill, that bill and some other bill.' I say 'Fine, what else would you like?' When they say 'What's your bottom line?' — 'Oh no, no. I want to hear from you. I want to hear what's important to you ... nothing's more important than anything else I'm just hear to listen.' Clearly something would be more important to me, but you would never know it. I learned that from people who have negotiated to buy things for four thousand years in the same way."

Schweitzer sees this cultural difference as a key to why the United States still fails to understand and negotiate well with many of the countries in the Middle East. Most of the time American politicians fly over to the region, hit four countries in one day, and then fly home and wonder why things didn't change. "It's something they will never know or understand because time is on the side of a bedouin. A bedouin will wait you out. A bedouin will stay in one place for three days, three weeks, three years, thirty years, three generations and they're not going to tell you what they really care about and they're going to wait until you play your cards. Once they see all of your cards and what's important to you, then and only then will they take some action.

"I can tell you this, if someone would like to negotiate something in the Middle East, send me. I've been there and I've been pretty successful at it. There are a lot of things I'm not great at. I'll be the first to tell you that. [There are] a lot of things I don't do very well, but I'm a pretty dang good negotiator. I learned a lot of that doing business negotiations in the Middle East."

While a private farm developer in Saudia Arabia, Schweitzer typically didn't negotiate a salary for his work but instead negotiated a share of the profit from the crops. It was a fail-safe business for the clients but put pressure on Schweitzer to make a farm produce. "I came in and said, 'Hey, I'll get the feasibility study approved. I'll buy the equipment. I'll build the farm. I'll grow the crop. You pay me nothing and I'll take a percentage of the crop.' So they had no risk. If the whole thing failed, they hadn't written a check, they hadn't put a dime into it, and they hadn't paid me anything. The only way it would be successful is if I successfully built the farm and grew the crop."

But Schweitzer always got paid. None of his farms failed. He ran into some glitches—late equipment, slow well diggers—but he always realized some sort of harvest. As a private farm developer, Schweitzer made about $90,000 a year.

18

Back in Montana

Before Schweitzer left for the Middle East, he fell in love. Her name was Nancy Hupp, and she was an undergraduate in botany. Their first date was either at a local sandwich shop in Bozeman, the Pickle Barrel (according to Brian), or a trip to look at farm machinery for sale (according to Nancy). In less than two years, in January of 1982, they were married. In May Nancy followed her ambitious husband to Saudi Arabia. The dairy was located about sixty miles south of Riyadh, in the center of the country.

Nancy doesn't give many interviews. In fact, the only full interview she has given went to Chuck Johnson in the summer of 2006. She told Johnson that, while in Saudi Arabia, by law she had to wear long dresses with sleeves that covered her arms down to her wrists. She also attended a reading group and a large women's luncheon. "I'm glad I was there," she told Johnson. "It was interesting, and the people are very nice. It's a beautiful country in its own way. And we got to see a lot of it from the farm."

According to Schweitzer, Nancy is the one who tempers his more flamboyant personality. "She's been a balancing act to me," he said.

Schweitzer doesn't consider himself a romantic. He's just not geared that way. But still some of his happiest days have been with Nancy. He talks fondly of "the times in our marriage when you're just completely, insanely in love, you can't be happier than just holding each other's hands and just reflecting on the world around you."

In 1986 Nancy became pregnant and the couple moved back to Montana, buying land in Whitefish. Their son Ben was born in September. Schweitzer kept working in the Middle East for a few more years, traveling back and forth between Whitefish and Saudi Arabia. And even after he'd settled down in Montana for good, his business in international agriculture continued. While in Saudi Arabia he had developed and patented a brand of alfalfa that grows well in the desert, and now he contracted with farmers in California and Washington to produce seed for the Middle East. He also continued his family's preoccupation with Simmental cattle, selling frozen embryos and semen to Latin America.

But not everything he touched turned to gold. He partnered with Alfa Laval and the World Bank to try to establish dairy farms on the impoverished Philippine island of Mindanao. The idea was to help farmers transition from date palms (a staple that was high in fat but low in protein) to forage crops and then provide each farmer with a few Holstein cows for milk. The farmers would bring the milk to a processing facility, which would then ship the milk around the country. "I was excited about it and I went over there and did a lot of soil work and gathered climatic data and knew what crops would grow at what elevations and where we would locate the dairy processing facility," he said.

But it was a dangerous place. Islamic extremists populated part of the island. "They routinely rounded up Westerners and cut their heads off. Everywhere I went I had guys with guns trying to protect me. And you know, frankly, it wasn't worth it. I'd love to change the world but I can't change anything if I get myself killed," Schweitzer said.

Schweitzer instead focused on Montana. On the farm in Whitefish, he began raising mint, a crop that was experiencing something of a resurgence, particularly in the Pacific Northwest. By the time Schweitzer began farming mint, a handful of farmers had already established mint operations around Whitefish, so Schweitzer not only began growing mint himself but also established a plant to distill mint oil from the raw leaves.

But land was expensive in the Flathead Valley, too expensive to make sense for farming, so Schweitzer began doing soil and climatic studies of eastern Washington and the Willamette Valley in Oregon, where mint had been grown successfully for years. He also had a hunch that mint could be grown in eastern Montana. He finally bought a large farm near Forsyth on the Yellowstone River, moving his mint operation there in the early 1990s. Schweitzer explained, "It's a risky business, mint is. The oil has to smell right. It's like people tasting your wine. The way you grow it, the kind of irrigation scheduling you have, the fertilizer you put on it, it all has an effect. And every area has a little bit different niche smell. The oil I grew in eastern Montana wasn't like western Montana oil. It was like central Oregon oil, which turned out to be a pretty good thing because that was the oil they were paying the most money for."

But the price of mint oil was, like so many other crops, at the whim of global commodities markets. And in the late 1990s, rumor had it that Wal-Mart had begun pressuring the three big American mint buyers (Colgate/Palmolive, Proctor and Gamble, and Wrigley's) to go overseas for manufacturing, thus lowering their overhead. Used to be, according to Schweitzer, those companies would contract with mint farmers for three years at a time, paying $18 a pound for mint oil. But they could buy mint in China for less than $7 a pound. In America you can't make a profit at that rate, so when things changed, Schweitzer got out: "We were flabbergasted. They had to know that this would put us out of business. Some farmers continued growing mint, but me, I don't need the practice." So he grew other crops, including soybeans.

In all, Schweitzer owned the farm in Forsyth for about ten years, selling it for roughly three times what he paid for it. As part of that deal, he also acquired a ranch in Hot Springs, Montana. After he was elected governor, he sold the ranch in Whitefish. He also bought four lots in a subdivision on Georgetown Lake, about an hour south of Butte. Georgetown Lake has seen an increase in development over the past decade, mostly in second and third homes, and so Schweitzer easily sold two of the lots. He's in the process of building a lakeshore home on the fourth. In the summer of 2007, he also bought a ranch in Avon, a small town near Helena.

Schweitzer isn't bashful when it comes to talking about his properties. "I like ranches," he said. "I like land. I like to kick dirt. I like to grow things. I like to look out across acres and know that . . . this is my piece of Montana."

19

A Politician, Born

In 1993 Schweitzer received a call from Senator Max Baucus's staff asking if he would accept an appointment to the Montana's Farm Services Agency state board, an organization that represents regional agriculture and is a liaison to the U.S. Department of Agriculture. The formal appointment comes from the secretary of agriculture, but the state's senior member of Congress provides nominations.

The offer took Schweitzer by surprise. He didn't really consider himself a Democrat so much as an Independent, but Baucus apparently didn't care about political affiliation. Schweitzer recalled, "He was just looking for bright, independent, passionate representatives of farm country. They were looking for a diverse group of people from outside of politics." Despite the fact that he'd "never been active or political," Schweitzer accepted and served on the board with Nancy Peterson and Bruce Nelson. (After Schweitzer became governor, he appointed Peterson as director of the Montana Department of Agriculture, and Nelson is now his chief of staff. In June of 2007 Peterson passed away after battling cancer for almost a year.)

While on the FSA board, Schweitzer was also appointed to the National Drought Task Force, which consulted with elected officials on public policy in dealing with drought. Between the two appointments Schweitzer began to develop an interest in public policy and public office.

In 1999 he met with the chair of the Montana Democratic Party, Bob Ream. "Once again, I didn't know what the heck I was thinking, but I decided to run for Congress," Schweitzer laughed. "I was just a regular citizen who said I think I've got some ideas that I'd like to contribute."

Ream told him that the Democrats were going to have a meeting in Helena to decide who was going to run for what office and that Schweitzer was welcome to attend. Though Schweitzer could see that the Democratic Party was more in line with his personal politics than the Republicans, he still didn't consider himself a mainstream Democrat: "I hadn't been somebody that had been identifiable politically. Most of the time I voted for Democrats, but I also voted for Republicans, and at times I still do. But you'd have to drag me to the ground and kick me in the ribs to get me to tell you who."

He still considers himself a bit of a party maverick. "I still don't drink all of the Kool-Aid. I drink some of the flavors, but not all of them."

In Helena it became pretty clear that he was an outsider looking in. Nancy Keenan, then superintendent of the Office of Public Instruction, was a favorite of the party for Congress against Republican Denny Rehburg. "I went to the meeting but I was under the impression that I wasn't going to run for Congress," Schweitzer said. "I was an outsider; I didn't have any chance there." It was also apparent that the Democrats had several candidates who wanted to run for governor. (Mark O'Keefe would eventually get the nomination but lose to Judy Martz.)

One of the Democrats at the meeting vying for Governor was 2007 state senate president, Mike Cooney, who had served in the state legislature and as secretary of state. Cooney didn't know Schweitzer before the meeting in Helena. "This fellow showed up at that meeting and very few people knew who he was. He stood up and introduced himself and said 'I'm going to run against Conrad Burns and I'm going to beat him,'" Cooney said. "It was a little bit curious that you had a room full of people who had been fairly active in the Democratic Party for several years and to have this fellow walk in out of nowhere and announce he was going to run for U.S. Senate."

Schweitzer was surprised no one at the meeting wanted to take on Burns in the Senate race. He had mulled it over and decided he would throw his hat in the ring: "I didn't know anything about this stuff. I had no idea how you would even go about filing to run for office."

Compared to other states, Montana's Democratic Party system for selecting candidates is fairly informal. In Massachusetts, for instance, potential candidates have to navigate a tough caucus system that begins in cities and towns where delegates are elected for specific candidates. Then the party endorsement is decided at the state convention. Several candidates are likely to run for major offices, but the party only endorses the one who received the most delegates at the convention.

In Montana, anyone can run for a state office. He or she simply announces he or she is running and then starts raising money. But fund-raising, developing a platform, getting your message out, that's where experience comes in handy. And it was all new ground for Schweitzer. Given that he had zero name recognition around Montana, he just decided to campaign like he was killing snakes.

Though Schweitzer wasn't a committed Democrat until he ran for Senate, his leanings were beginning to surface a year or two earlier. Dusty Deschamps, a lawyer in Missoula, ran on the Democratic ticket for Congress in 1998 against incumbent Republican Rick Hill. During the campaign Schweitzer called Deschamps out of the blue. "He was his typical self," Deschamps said. "All hyped up, excited, and full of ideas." Schweitzer had some notions for Deschamps on the race against Hill. He was paying attention to his new party, to the political scene, and wanted to help a Democrat win.

"I didn't know quite what to make of him," Deschamps said. "My initial shock was tempered quite a bit by his intelligence and enthusiasm and good ideas." When Deschamps heard Schweitzer was running against Burns, he wasn't surprised at all. "Brian happens to be one of those types that has the enthusiasm and the energy and the willingness to work to make it happen."

Gary Buchanan, Ted Schwinden's former commerce director, first ran into Schweitzer in 1999 when Schweitzer was in fund-raising mode. "The first time I met Brian Schweitzer, this whirlwind of energy came piling into my office and ended up leaving with a check," he said. "I was very impressed." Buchanan considers himself a moderate, and likes Schweitzer—the energy, the ideas, the gumption, and what he calls raw charisma. "He comes into a room and you sure as hell know he's there," he said.

Meanwhile, Schweitzer wasn't quite prepared for what he was getting into. "It's like getting on a boat and going to a new land. You really don't know what it looks like until you get there. I had a lot of things to learn."

Schweitzer figured he'd just hop in his pickup and drive around Montana and stop in at stores, cafés and feed lots, shaking hands, listening to people's ideas, and giving them a few of his. "I did that for about five solid months, and I bet I still didn't have 1 percent name identification. If you would have gone back to one of those stores two days later and said 'Hey do you know who Brian Schweitzer is?' they would have said 'Nope, I don't know that fellow.'" He realized he was going to have to go to newspaper, radio, and television ads. "Just meeting people by the gas pump or stopping to help them fix their flat tire—that doesn't get the job done. There's a process and it all takes money and that was the daunting task," Schweitzer said. "When somebody said to me, 'Well if you're running for the U.S. Senate, you're going to have to raise a couple of million dollars,' I thought to myself, 'Who in the heck would give me $2 million?'"

He was going to have to get thousands of people to write him checks. That meant developing a system for presenting himself to voters and donors. "I couldn't afford ads early and so it was a Godsend when the pharmaceutical companies started running ads in Montana against me, with my picture attached."

National interest groups like Citizens for Better Medicare and the U.S. Chamber of Commerce funded ads against Schweitzer and his stand against high-dollar prescription drugs in America. For Schweitzer's first campaign stunt, in September of 1999 (and in an early indication of his populist leanings), he loaded up a bus full of Kalispell senior citizens and drove them across the border into Canada to buy prescription drugs. Pharmaceutical companies were charging nearly twice as much in America as in Canada and Mexico for exactly the same drugs. It didn't make any sense that these companies were lining their pockets off the sick and the elderly, he said. He meant to draw attention to the problem and try to shame Congress into addressing the issue. Other politicians around the country were soon following his example. "It was a road map for every senior who lived close to the border to show them what they ought to be doing," he said.

When the pharmaceutical companies started running anti-Schweitzer ads in Montana, no one really knew who he was. But all that soon changed. It seemed the drug companies didn't really understand Montana. They seemed to think that negative ads run by big businesses and outside interest groups might work. But all they did was give people a reason to follow Schweitzer. "Really it was the pharmaceutical companies that launched my political career," he said. The way Schweitzer sees it now, people watched those ads and thought, "I don't know who that guy is, but if they don't like him, maybe I do."

Behind the scenes, however, Democratic strategists didn't understand why he was putting so much behind the prescription-drug issue. They told him the issue was about fourteenth on the list of what people cared about. But it was important to Schweitzer and he knew it was important to Montana. Maybe only one person in fifty cares about the cost of prescription drugs, Schweitzer said. "But that might be the most important one person out of fifty. Those are our parents and grandparents. Those are folks who have raised families, and all their lives played by the rules, and now the rules have shifted. Now they can't afford to buy their medicine and live a healthy and productive life." It was a populist stance, looking out for those in need. "It affects everybody. There are very few families that are not touched by this inequity. Once they found out that they were being effectively ripped off by American industry, then people got it."

The way he attacked the pharmaceutical companies was, in hindsight, a stroke of brilliance and gave an early glimpse into his political savvy. When a little guy takes on big business and gets them to respond, it means attention, and attention is crucial for a political upstart.

Though the drug runs over the border brought him attention and remain something people remember about Schweitzer, he still doesn't think it put him in the spotlight. But it did kick off a campaign that continually pitted him as the little guy going against Burns, a strong incumbent senator with a growing amount of power in Washington, D.C.

The race between Burns and Schweitzer was fairly bitter. At one point Burns accused Schweitzer of illegally bringing pesticides across the border from Canada, a claim Burns never validated with proof. "They made it up from scratch," Schweitzer said. "Accused me of a felony and made it up from scratch."

Usually a challenger runs a negative campaign against the incumbent, Schweitzer said. But he claims his campaign against Burns was clean. Not to say he didn't pull a stunt or two. Like the day he showed up at a press conference at the capitol in Helena and dumped $47,000 in cash across the floor, pointing out that this was the amount Burns had taken from tobacco lobbyists. "What is it that the tobacco industry does for Montana?" he asked. "Do we grow tobacco here? Do we roll cigarettes here? Do we have people employed that manufacture cigarettes? No, no, no. Mostly [the tobacco industry] creates health problems for families in Montana. So why the heck would anybody be tight or in bed with the tobacco industry?"

Schweitzer claims Burns investigated him and sent "suits" around to county courthouses in the state, trying to dig up dirt. They called old friends trying to get an edge. Schweitzer wasn't ready for that. "I guess I was prepared to talk about the issues and maybe compare my ideas versus somebody else's, but just to have folks make up stuff . . . that's a little tough. But, ah, I've got thick skin."

Schweitzer pointed to Burns's record, which he said demonstrated how he'd lost touch with Montana, voting for big corporations over regular Montanans. He continually accused him of paying more attention to lobbyists, who filled his pockets, than the needs of his state. (A claim that would later be supported by Burns's connection with the Abramoff scandal, although in early 2008, the Justice Department investigation into Burns's involvement with Abramoff was completed without any charges being filed.)

Throughout the race Schweitzer steadily chipped away at Burns's lead. This farmer from Whitefish, a political nobody, was actually looking like he'd have a shot at upsetting the most popular Republican senator in Montana's history.

In September of 2000 Schweitzer was twenty points behind Burns in the polling. By the end of October it was too close to call. The national parties began dumping money into the race. The Democrats saw their chance to gain an important seat in the closely divided Senate. The Republicans desperately wanted to hold that edge. Come election night, early results showed Schweitzer ahead, and two major news stations actually called the race in his favor. But he knew it wasn't done. Finally, about 2:30 in the morning, it was clear that he'd lost. Burns beat Schweitzer 51 to 47 percent. "I called Senator Burns and congratulated him and, you know, told him I was looking forward to him being our senator for the next six years," Schweitzer said.

After the election he said he went back to "raising crops and cattle and kids." And even though he lost, he said he "learned a heck of a lot," like how to listen to the people of Montana: "Folks have notions, they have ideas, and if you give them a chance, they'll unload. I'm a pretty dang good listener."

He also learned how to fund-raise. "In a political campaign you have to raise money," he said. It's not an aspect of politics people like, but right now those are the rules. Schweitzer has said he'll no longer take any money from political action committees. Instead, he has to convince thousands of people to be a part of his campaign, to contribute as individuals. Schweitzer says he's done it mainly by building a large grassroots organization in the state. This has allowed him to touch many average Montanans who may have never given money to a candidate in their lives.

In the race, Burns out-earned Schweitzer more than two to one. According to information complied by OpenSecrets.org, Burns raised about $5.2 million to Schweitzer's $2.1 million. Burns's campaign was 43 percent funded by PACs. His top contributions were from businesses, such as AT&T, Lockheed Martin, and Microsoft Corporation. Schweitzer's campaign was 17 percent funded by PACs. Top campaign contributors for Schweitzer were more standard PACs, such as the AFL-CIO, National Committee for an Effective Congress, and several labor unions.

Individual contributions between the two campaigns were nearly identical. Schweitzer was funded 55 percent by individuals and Burns 52 percent. Schweitzer had 1,832 individual contributions. Burns received 2,350. Schweitzer collected 32 percent of his individual donations from in-state donors, while Burns collected 35 percent in state.

Schweitzer told me that many of the out-of-state donations came after the race began to look competitive and started gaining national attention. People contributed to him because they wanted a Democrat to win, not because he'd asked them to.

In this first race Schweitzer says he took PAC money because he was a newcomer. "When I ran for the U.S. Senate, I'd never been elected to anything [outside college]. I was completely outside the system."

That meant he had to learn the system and play catch up. He knew he was going to have to raise a lot of money, and that meant political action committees. "All you're doing is following the pack in front of you and hoping you catch up with them," he said.

However, his view on PAC money changed with one event. Paul Wellstone and his wife, Sheila, along with their daughter, Marcia, died tragically in a plane crash on October 25, 2002. Wellstone was a popular and outspoken senator from Minnesota. He was a progressive who worked against the lobbying establishment in Washington. Schweitzer looked up to Wellstone. "I didn't always agree with him, but I became an admirer of his. He would be completely comfortable standing alone," Schweitzer said. He specifically admired the fact that Wellstone wouldn't take PAC money. Like Schweitzer, Wellstone felt that special interests had too much influence in the lawmaking process. "When his plane went down that day, I thought we need more people like him. That was the day I decided to run for governor and the day I decided not to take PAC money," he said.

20

The Governor's Race

After his loss to Burns in 2000, Schweitzer kept showing up in the news, writing columns critical of power deregulation in Montana, and promoting prescription-drug reform at the federal level. In the *Billings Gazette* Schweitzer was identified as a Montana columnist and a Whitefish farmer. He wrote passionately about the issues that he would come to champion as a governor, particularly the influence of lobbyists in Washington, D.C. In a column about the cost of prescription drugs, he wrote, "The fight is not over. On one side you have the drug companies, their billions of dollars, a bought Congress and a pack of lies. On the other side, we have few resources, no Congress, a farmer from Whitefish, a bunch of determined Montanans and the truth."

Schweitzer kept himself in the public eye, and in 2004 Chuck Johnson, a bureau chief for the newspaper conglomerate Lee Enterprises, wrote, "When prominent current and former Democratic officeholders began sniffing around in 2002 and 2003 to decide whether they should run against unpopular Republican Governor Judy Martz in 2004, they quickly learned that Schweitzer already enjoyed a huge advantage. Heading into 2004, Schweitzer, for all practical purposes, had the Democratic nomination sewn up in terms of organization and access to money."

But Schweitzer, by his account at least, wasn't initially set on running for governor. He told Johnson in 2001 that he was thinking of running for something, but just didn't know what. His comments were in response to then Montana Republican chairman Matt Denny, who was pointing to a quote from Schweitzer in the *Choteau Acantha* to the effect that he wouldn't run. Denny, likely because he knew Schweitzer would be a powerful opponent, planned to hold Schweitzer to his pledge. Schweitzer replied, "People all over the state of Montana are encouraging me to run for Congress, public service commissioner, or governor. I have not decided to run. Before Matt Denny knows and the Republican Party knows, first my wife's got to say it's OK. Number two, I've got to finish calving. Number three, I've got to get a crop in."

But as Martz's approval ratings continued to plummet, Schweitzer looked more and more like the clear choice to take up the Democrat's flag. By early 2003 it was obvious that Schweitzer would be running for governor.

In lieu of Martz, four other Republican candidates stepped up to the plate: Pat Davison, a Billings businessman; Bob Brown, secretary of state; Ken Miller, a state legislator; and Tom Keating, a former state legislator. It quickly became clear that the primary race was going to be between Davison and Brown. It would be a heated contest and ultimately divisive for the Republicans. When Brown announced his plan to run for governor in July (before Martz had made her decision whether or not to seek reelection), rumors around Helena maintained that Martz was upset and so supported Davison, a more-conservative Republican.

A student at Connecticut College, Christopher Devine, dissected the 2004 Montana gubernatorial primary and subsequent general election race in his honors thesis. Devine's thesis looked at gubernatorial races in states where the party of the winning candidate differed from the party the state voted for in the 2004 presidential election. (In 2004, Montana voted Schweitzer into office, while overwhelmingly supporting George Bush in the presidential election.)

Of the Montana Republican gubernatorial primary, Devine wrote in his thesis: "The contest ultimately degenerated into a very negative exchange, in which both major candidates cast their opponent as untrustworthy, dishonest, unethical, and irresponsible." In the June primary, Brown garnered 39 percent of the vote, while Davison received 23 percent, Miller 22 percent, and Keating 16 percent. But in order to win the nomination, Brown had spent nearly 90 percent of his campaign finances, leaving only $44,000 for the general election—less than a tenth of Schweitzer's funds.

After the primary, Republicans failed to gel behind Brown. In a Montana State University–Billings poll conducted less than a month before the election, an astounding 57 percent of Republican voters said they were still undecided. The same poll showed Schweitzer leading Brown 43 percent to 28 percent. Brown later told Devine that he believed the people who had supported Davison and the other primary candidates withheld support in the general election. "I think a fair number of the real, solid movement conservatives left us [the Republican gubernatorial ticket] blank, they just didn't vote for us," Brown told Devine. "I didn't have the full strength of my own side behind me, because of that divisive primary."

Schweitzer would have an easier time of his primary. His challenger, Gallatin County commissioner John Vincent, and his running mate, Mary Sexton, a county commissioner from Teton County, never materialized as a real threat. In 2007 Sexton said the main reason Vincent ran was to illuminate a number of issues they felt were important to Montana— primarily Montana's tax structure and how it affected economic growth. Vincent's presence in the race gave reason for these issues to be debated before the primary, which Schweitzer won easily. It turned out that Vincent and Schweitzer agreed on most issues. However, Vincent supported a sales tax to fund education and roll back property taxes.

Schweitzer didn't support a sales tax. Vincent also touted his long legislative experience. He had served sixteen years in the Montana house, as well four years as a Gallatin County commissioner. Vincent tried to score points by criticizing Schweitzer on his lack of experience. But Schweitzer had developed a canned response any time a reporter asked him about Vincent's criticisms: "John Vincent's a good guy with a lot of experience, and I look forward to hearing his ideas." Schweitzer otherwise kept his mouth shut about his primary opponent, coming out of the primary with a healthy campaign fund of nearly $500,000.

There are clear advantages to being an outsider, to not having a political track record your opponents can exploit. You can paint yourself as a reformer, as someone unpolluted by a process that most everyone (particularly in the West) finds distasteful. You're going to be the one to bring change to the system. Somehow, no matter how often we hear it, we still want to believe it. And coming out of an unpopular administration, Montana seemed particularly open to the notion of political reform.

Schweitzer vowed to not kowtow to the political machine. He didn't take money from political action committees, saying he didn't want to be beholden to any interest group. He shunned lobbyists. Instead of talking about ways to get big industry into Montana, Schweitzer talked up the need to stimulate small businesses. He talked about fighting for hunting and fishing access for sportsmen around the state. He promoted a health-care program for small businesses and advocated more money for education, calling it the great equalizer between the classes. He was bearing the flag of the average Montanan in a decidedly populist campaign. "Schweitzer said his lack of experience allowed him to transcend traditional partisan loyalties and do what was best for the state, regardless of entrenched interests," Devine wrote.

His decision to pick John Bohlinger as a running mate—a Republican state senator—was meant to be a clear indication of his nontraditional approach to politics. He would be a bridge builder.

21

John Bohlinger

During the summer of 2003, Schweitzer traveled around Montana looking for a running mate. He talked with people from all over the state and all walks of life. He interviewed Chris Junghans, a high school teacher and college professor in Bozeman. Junghans had also worked for Republicans, crafting policy under George H.W. Bush and as communication director for the Montana Republican Party. Schweitzer also talked to Katie Hanning, the president of the Great Falls chapter of the National Association of Women in Construction. After nearly forty potential candidates, ultimately, he chose John Bohlinger, a respected and moderate Republican politician from Billings.

A native Montanan (his family owned a women's clothing store in Billings, which he later ran), Bohlinger greets you with a warm smile, grasping your hand with both of his. In an article written just after Schweitzer and Bohlinger won the election, reporter Jennifer McKee described the new lieutenant governor as a lawmaker who "crusaded for causes not always associated with the Republican Party. In the 2003 session he had unsuccessfully promoted a plan to boost spending on public education by increasing taxes on cigarettes and video gambling. He also urged using car rental tax dollars to pay for the state park system." His priorities reflected those issues that were close to his heart. He tried to get a sales tax passed that would lower income and property taxes while still maintaining programs for the poor and elderly. McKee wrote, "Dressed in his characteristic bow tie, Bohlinger often pitched his bills by quoting from the Book of Matthew: 'I was hungry and you gave me food, I was thirsty and you gave me drink.'"

Bohlinger's faith is clearly an essential part of his life. "I've always said the way you spend your money is a reflection of your values," he said in 2007. Along with the obvious and often remarked-upon gesture toward bipartisanship, it's hard not to speculate that Schweitzer chose Bohlinger, at least in part, because of a shared commitment to Catholicism. (They have one significant point of difference, however: Schweitzer is pro-choice while Bohlinger is pro-life.) In any case 2004 marked the first time in Montana's history that a Democrat and Republican ran on the same ticket.

The two met in May of 2003 at a mutual friend's office in Billings. "In that first meeting we discovered that in spite of the fact that I'm a Republican and he's a Democrat, we share a lot of the same values," Bohlinger said, pointing specifically to the fact that they both shared the same Catholic faith.

Humble and soft spoken, Bohlinger stands in marked contrast to Schweitzer, the aggressive and confident rancher. When I first met Bohlinger, his wife, Bette,was fighting leukemia. A mutual friend asked after her health, and Bohlinger began to tear up. "She's much stronger than I am," he said then. (Bette eventually lost her fight with leukemia in January 2006. The disease had gone into remission and then reemerged again in December 2005.)

From his first meeting with Schweitzer in 2003, they began an informal discussion. Bohlinger knew Schweitzer was looking for a running mate but didn't think he was being considered. Then in November of 2003, Schweitzer came to Billings for another visit. According to Bohlinger, Schweitzer said, "You know, John, I've had a number of your legislative colleagues suggest to me that you'd be a great running mate and I'm inclined to agree."

Bohlinger told Schweitzer that he would have to meet with his family before giving him an answer. Bette was puzzled as to why her husband would consider such a move at an age when most people retire. (When Schweitzer came calling, Bohlinger was sixty-seven.) But Bohlinger decided that he wanted to be involved in policy from the governor's office, in advocating for better education, human services, and a cleaner environment. He wanted to have a seat at the table. He also shared with Schweitzer a view that a bridge between the Democrat and Republican parties in Montana needed to be built. "I think that public policy is crafted from the middle," he said. He felt that this could be an administration that worked on both sides of the aisle.

Republicans took less generously to the notion of adding Bohlinger to the ticket. Christopher Devine wrote that Bob Brown particularly felt betrayed by the decision. Bohlinger and Brown were friends, and Brown had thought he could count on his support for his campaign.

Bohlinger insisted that he was still part of the Republican Party. According to Devine, he explained, "I feel that it would be disingenuous of us [the incoming administration] to suddenly announce to people that now that we are elected I'm becoming a Democrat."

Chuck Johnson wrote in November 2004 of the cool reception Bohlinger began to receive from his fellow Republicans. Senator Dan McGee of Laurel was frustrated that Bohlinger had campaigned against some Republican legislative candidates. He told Bohlinger that people felt betrayed by his decision to join Schweitzer. "I'm sorry you feel betrayed," Bohlinger told his Yellowstone County colleague, according to Johnson.

"It's not me," McGee said. "There's thousands of people who feel betrayed."

For Bohlinger's part the decision to join Schweitzer wasn't about politics; it was about Montana. "I think we both came to an understanding about the need to bridge this gap that exists between the political parties," Bohlinger said. "My first impression (of Schweitzer) is one I still hold. My first impression was that he's a very bright guy. Smart as can be. He is very energetic. One who truly has Montana's interest at heart." And while they don't agree on everything, Bohlinger said, as in a good marriage, they "disagree without being disagreeable."

Schweitzer did his best to emphasize this bipartisanship during the race. An Associated Press article quoted him after he and Bohlinger officially filed for the election. "People have talked about building bridges, people have talked about coming to Helena to build bridges to bring the parties together," he said, standing next to Bohlinger. "Guess what? We've poured the concrete, we've bolted together the planks, we've put the steel over the top. The bridge is built."

The move also shrewdly took away one of Brown's platforms. Brown had been widely known and respected as a legislator. An affable and intelligent moderate, at the time of the election, he had spent nearly thirty years in Montana politics, working toward consensus across the aisles. It was almost impossible to find a politician who had something bad to say about him. But after Bohlinger came on with Schweitzer, Brown could no longer point to his bipartisanship as a clear and unique asset. Brown told Devine, "[When] anyone would say, 'Bob Brown's pretty skilled as a bridge builder; he's reached out to groups and organizations and people that most Republicans can't reach out to,' Schweitzer would look at them and say, "What do you mean Bob Brown's a bridge builder? Heck, my running mate's a Republican.' He trumped that."

22

The Governor's Race Again

Schweitzer was fortunate in his timing. In the wake of Judy Martz's unpopularity, with the state's Republican Party in disarray, Schweitzer gained momentum as the campaign progressed. Christopher Devine wrote, "Schweitzer's energetic campaigning helped make up for his government inexperience by familiarizing him with voters' concerns and expectations. In terms of leadership, it also conveyed to voters that he had the enthusiasm and vigor necessary to take on the imposing task of reforming state government."

In 2004 Schweitzer told AP reporter Bob Anez that a good governor "needs to know personally all the people that pull the ropes in Montana. It's about building personal relationships."

His opponent, Bob Brown, had a more relaxed demeanor, perhaps temperamentally unsuited to an aggressive campaign. He often referred to himself as the "workhorse" and Schweitzer as the "show horse." According to Devine, Brown described fund-raising as "the most unpleasant feeling" and "the most sickening aspect of politics."

A couple of years later, Brown told me Schweitzer's energy and demeanor all represented change to Montanans. Many people "thought Montana was kind of stuck in the mud." Schweitzer recognized that people were ready for change. In an article by Bob Anez, Brown characterized the race as a "pretty clear contest between a flamboyant showman with a gift for finding the political hot buttons and a public servant who's been involved positively, constructively, and effectively in our state for many years, and has a record to prove it."

James Lopach, political scientist from the University of Montana, told Devine, "[Schweitzer] projected the image of being an engaged, vigorous candidate committed to making change on behalf of the state. And Bob [Brown] did not do it."

Schweitzer also continued to effectively tie Brown to the Martz administration, even though Brown had been elected separately to his post as secretary of state. It could be seen as a mistake that Brown, perhaps trying not to alienate other members of his party, never explicitly criticized Martz. "He sort of suggested he might do some things differently [than her], but he never really took her on as an issue," Chuck Johnson told Devine.

Schweitzer, meanwhile, continued to emphasize his outsider role. In one debate, he said, "Mr. Brown, you've been a part of this group that has been running this government now for thirty years. Why should we stay the course with you?"

When the election rolled around, Schweitzer was in a commanding lead in the polls, though he didn't slow up campaigning. As he told the people at a rally in Hamilton, in October, "I'm going to keep running like we're behind."

In the end Schweitzer beat Brown 51 to 47 percent, with a small percentage going to the Green and Libertarian candidates.

23

Politics and Leadership

How does one judge a politician?

While I was still an undergraduate at the University of Montana, I attended a leadership conference in Washington, D.C., hosted by then vice president Al Gore. In the shadow of monuments dedicated to the greatest leaders of our country, we discussed the idea of leadership, the value of it, what it means, and how it's done. Congress wasn't in session, and so I was able to take a chair on the floor of the House. I stared up at the ceiling, awed. This was the heart of our government, a room where laws were introduced, where wars were started, where decisions were made that affected the lives of three hundred million people.

But the most valuable part of the weekend was a stroll to the Capitol with Oklahoma congressman Steve Largent, Pro Football Hall of Famer and former player for the Seattle Seahawks. In our few minutes together, he talked about the value of humility, as well as the importance of cooperation. Even though the squabbling in Congress makes for good headlines, most legislators work together quite easily; they even like each other. The key, Largent said as we walked, is humility. A good leader

94

doesn't think he's got the only answer but gives other people a voice and is humble enough to give other ideas strong consideration. He's always first to apologize when tensions are high and feelings are hurt.

As I chased Schweitzer around Montana, I kept thinking about that weekend in D.C. Was Schweitzer a real leader? An honest and earnest proponent of bipartisanship? Montana is full of extraordinary men and women, farmers, business owners, physicians, contractors, none of whom have run for public office, none of whom have aspired to be on television. I asked Schweitzer what set him apart from other Montanans.

"Not a dang thing and that's why I'm successful. I think like they do and I speak like they do. Whether I'm speaking from a podium or whether I'm speaking at a kitchen table or whether we're talking over a phone, it's not a lot different. It's not a skill but a non-skill. My non-skill is that I don't speak like a politician does. I don't speak off of talking points. I don't stay on a script. People ask me a straight question I give them a straight answer. People ask me a question and I know they're not going to like the answer, I tell them anyway. I just lay it out."

It's an education, watching Brian Schweitzer with his dog, Jag. They have a real attachment. The border collie always knows where his owner is. He's always got his eyes on the governor. But in a crowded room, unless he's being asked to perform by Schweitzer, the dog gets nervous. Especially with kids, Jag can be skittish, capable of snapping at a grabby child. One of Schweitzer's staffers was particularly on edge at a Democratic rally in Kalispell, just prior to the 2006 elections. He and I stood off to the side with Schweitzer's bodyguard, watching the governor move from person to person, shaking hands. When a group of kids made a beeline for Jag, the staffer grabbed the dog and whisked him outside for a walk. I've had the feeling, particularly at events that Schweitzer seems less than excited about, that both he and Jag are keeping an eye on the door.

It's perhaps Brian Schweitzer's Achilles' heel that he too often comes across as distracted, less than utterly focused. With about a week left in the 2007 legislative session, he visited California to attend a fund-raising event for his 2008 reelection bid. While there he appeared on the HBO show *Real Time with Bill Maher.* During the 2007 session, Schweitzer was less of a presence than in the 2005 session, said Mike Cooney, who was the president of the senate during the 2007 session. Cooney said he encouraged Schweitzer to take a step back from being constantly involved with the legislature during the session. In 2005, Cooney said Schweitzer was always around and though it wasn't a distraction, Cooney thought it was unnecessary.

"In 07 he ended up staying more away from the legislature and let the legislature be the legislature and not feel the constant presence of the governor looking over their shoulder," Cooney said.

However, Chuck Johnson told me Schweitzer traveled more during a legislative session than any other governor he had covered.

Charles Mahtesian, editor of *The Almanac of American Politics,* said, "A governor like him in a state of Montana has to be very vigilant of not falling into the stereotypes that will be used against him." For Schweitzer to maintain his national image and progress, according to Mahtesian, he has to be careful not to overlook winning his 2008 reelection bid. He has to be careful to not appear like he's getting "too big for his britches."

24

His First Session

While Brian Schweitzer has attracted attention from the national press for his charisma, chutzpah, and innovative ideas with regard to energy, his legacy on the local level will largely depend on how he fares with the legislature.

Montana's legislature meets every two years for ninety days. The politicians converge on the small city of Helena to wrangle over budgets, introduce bills, amend bills in committee, reject bills, give interviews on the Capitol steps, and occasionally turn bills into laws. As with most state legislatures, Montana's politicians are a mishmash of attorneys, ranchers, doctors, farmers, and businessmen, all with varying degrees of education and talent. Optimists would say it's always about elected officials working together to get important measures passed. But a more cynical eye might compare the proceedings to a no-holds-barred boxing match slopping around in a cattle yard. The delegates sling crap at each other for a few months before grudgingly accepting a truce.

It's the governor's first job to work as efficiently and, hopefully, as amiably as possible with this second branch of state government.

In 2005 Schweitzer entered his first session with the luxury of a $300 million budget surplus and his party in control of both the house and the senate. By most accounts he did pretty well. He worked on priority bills relating to education spending, ethanol, and lower taxes for small businesses. His proposed budget had a $117 million increase in spending over Martz's last budget, and, while Republicans complained hard about his unwillingness to give back some of the surplus to taxpayers, he made good use of the money.

Notably, as mandated by a Montana Supreme Court decision, the 2005 legislature needed to more adequately fund K–12 education. It became the central issue and the cause of a special session in December. From the very beginning of the regular session, Schweitzer said education could be adequately funded without raising taxes. The question wasn't whether or not money should be pumped into education; the question was how *much* money, and where it was to be spent.

Education funding in Montana is confusing, done as it is partially on an enrollment basis. Schools with stable or growing student bodies have less trouble with it than schools with dwindling numbers. When the state doesn't come through with adequate funds, local property taxes have to make up the difference. Schweitzer and Republicans wanted to fund education in 2005 in such a way so that schools weren't forced to go to local homeowners for more money.

The sailing wasn't always smooth. In the regular session the legislature put $80 million into K–12 education for the coming two years. The Montana Quality Education Coalition wanted about twice as much money, but Schweitzer said the amount was a compromise with education advocacy groups and lawmakers. Schweitzer had voiced disapproval of a bill introduced by his own party that would have potentially raised property taxes by about $91 million. The past decade, schools had been forced to raise local taxes to make up for a short fall in state funding. "Some are suggesting we do that again," he told the Associated Press. "I didn't support it in the last ten years so it's unlikely I would support it now."

The special session began on December 14, 2005, after Schweitzer felt the legislature had found a solution. The session was predicted to last four days, but lawmakers got the work done in two. Schweitzer was able to get his funding solution pushed through quickly. In the end the legislature put $71 million more into schools and $125 million into the employee pension fund.

A conspicuous success for Schweitzer was his ability to get Republicans to vote his way in the split house. After the special session Chuck Johnson wrote that Schweitzer showed his "prowess" as a governor. "During the 2004 campaign, some wondered how the greenhorn Schweitzer would deal with the intricacies of the Legislature. The verdict so far: Just fine, thank you. Working with Democratic legislative leaders, Schweitzer and his staff know how to count votes and, when necessary, apply a little pork here and some raw political muscle there to grease bills through."

After all was said and done, government spending was up, taxes were either stable or had been reduced (some small businesses had seen their bills reduced or eliminated with a reworked business-equipment tax), and Montana still had money in the bank.

Schweitzer didn't get everything he wanted. He lost the battle to get money appropriated toward a review of state government spending. He also wasn't able to get an ethics bill passed that would have prevented lawmakers from becoming lobbyists until they were out of office for two years.

Johnson summed up Schweitzer's first session by saying that he "steered through bills promoting ethanol production, wind power, tax breaks to lure movies filmed here and country-of-origin labeling. He ruled out tax hikes and balanced the budget without them, although that wasn't hard with the surplus. . . . He eliminated property taxes on equipment for some businesses. He proved deft at lobbying individual Republicans, despite his oft-frigid dealings with GOP leaders."

Democratic senator Jim Elliott said that during Schweitzer's first session, Democratic lawmakers tried to protect Schweitzer as much as they could. "One thing that you want to do if you're the majority party and the governor is of your party is that you want to protect your governor." Cooney agreed with Elliot. "Anytime a new governor comes in everybody cuts that governor a little bit of slack."

25

The Economy

In his interview with Charlie Rose, Schweitzer was quick to take credit for Montana's blooming economy. Rose said to Schweitzer: "Tell me your political profile. Let's talk about economics. You say you'll never raise taxes, you'll always cut taxes."

Schweitzer responded: "Ah I wouldn't say that. I will say that I'll try and cut taxes whenever I can. I'll try to make government more efficient, I'll try and grow Montana's economy. . . . I'm attracting new businesses to come to Montana so our economy is booming. . . . I bring small businesses and big businesses. . . . Why build an office next door to the office you have right now? Why not build one in Montana? . . . I'm growing Montana's economy." And it's true that in 2007 Montana's bond rating was improved for the first time in twenty-six years. "You don't build the greatest number of jobs in the history of the state with the chief executive sitting on his hind end in Helena," Schweitzer said. "Everywhere I go, I talk about Montana."

But the ebb and flow of trends probably has a lot to do with Montana's natural attractiveness and growth, something Schweitzer is quick to promote. The entire region has been experiencing an unprecedented economic heyday. "People are moving to the Rocky Mountain West in large numbers and they're not moving there for the old reasons," Schweitzer told Charlie Rose. "They're not moving there for the metals in the mountains. . . . They're moving there for quality of life. . . . We've got the most remarkable places left on the planet to raise a family, start a business, build a community."

Economist and director of the O'Connor Center for the Rocky Mountain West at the University of Montana, Larry Swanson agrees. People are making a quality-of-life decision when they move to the region, but in the process they're also making a real economic impact. Particularly in the arenas of health care and construction (the building industry's income in Montana in 2000 was about $1.1 billion; in 2005 it was nearly $1.5 billion), Montana has become one of the more dynamic economies in America, as evidenced by a 2007 unemployment rate of around 2 percent. According to Swanson, Montana is actually heading toward a scenario where there will be more jobs than people to fill them. In the next four years, large numbers of baby boomers will begin retiring. The result will be a decrease in the amount of people in the workforce.

No single politician can take credit for the state's growth. But to keep us on the same path, an educated and skilled workforce is vital, Swanson said. In that regard Schweitzer's promotion of education will help train a future workforce, something to fill the demand in Montana. His energetic promotion of Montana has also been important.

Another key to the state's economic security is Schweitzer's ability to craft a solid budget, said Mike Cooney. "I think Governor Schweitzer has done a tremendous amount to keep Montana's financial house in order." In the past, Montana has got in trouble by passing state budgets that weren't fiscally sound. "Any monkey can create a balanced budget," he said. But structurally balanced budgets are harder to craft.

The difference between the two kinds of budget is pretty simple. A structurally sound budget doesn't allocate one-time funds to ongoing costs, Cooney said. Schweitzer has avoided doing that in both the 2005 and 2007 budgets. "Schweitzer's done his homework and really made some tough decisions to avoid being tempted to go down that road." This, along with the growth in the state and recent increase in oil production, have been key reasons why Montana's economy has been so good, Cooney said.

In his second State of the State address, Schweitzer told the legislature, "In my last [State of the State] speech, I proclaimed to you, 'Montana is open for business.' Do you remember? And, boy, are we open for business. During the last twenty-four months, we have created more than twenty-four thousand jobs. . . . Our unemployment is the lowest in history—2.8 percent.

"There are more people working in Montana today than at any time in the history of Montana," he added. "Montana is open for business and on the move."

26

The Second Session

For someone who enjoys watching regional politics, arenas often more similar to eight-man football than, say, the NFL they play in Washington, the 2007 legislative session was a fascinating study, filled with gaffes and blunders, indeed, but also energized by earnestness and real belief. After not controlling anything in Helena 2005, the Republicans won control of the Montana house and came into 2007 geared for battle. They refused for much of the session to bring key budget bills to the floor for debate. In negotiations the Republicans demanded Schweitzer and the Democrats give ground, all the while calling Schweitzer a bully and dictator.

Republicans had their slim majority in the house while the Democrats held the senate with a 26 to 24 majority. (The 2006 elections actually made it a tie in the senate, but moderate Republican Sam Kitzenberg, who was in the middle of his four-year term, switched parties after the election. He said he wanted to see Schweitzer's agenda make it through the legislature.) House Republicans elected starkly conservative Scott Sales from Bozeman as their speaker. Sales came out of the box saying that his party had lost its way and that he was planning a conservative agenda to show Republicans could still be counted on to promote smaller government and family values.

When Schweitzer submitted his budget proposal, Sales was determined to pare it down, disliking Schweitzer's proposed increase in state spending. The surplus for the new budget was now projected to be more than $1 billion, the bulk of which Schweitzer meant to see go to education, state prisons, and public retirement programs, all of which were in need of substantial amounts of revenue. A key part of his education package was the promotion of all-day kindergarten. He planned to increase state spending by $334 million, while giving a $400 property-tax rebate to homeowners and cutting the business-equipment tax. He also planned to squirrel $100 million away in a rainy-day fund.

Sales had other ideas. "I'm a fiscal conservative," he told reporter Jennifer McKee, "and the majority of the Republican side is, too. We're certainly going to be taking a hard line on a lot of [Schweitzer's proposed budget] growth. It's just not realistic." Sales and many of the Republicans advocated for permanent property-tax reductions. They believed that the surplus was made on the backs of Montana property owners, and that it should go back to them. They needed relief, Sales told reporters. "We are going to try to bring some sanity back to the budget process," he told the Associated Press.

Democrat Jim Elliott believes the Republican leadership in the house to have been extreme. Scott Sales refused to schedule bills for debate and consistently pushed Schweitzer for permanent tax breaks before he would let a budget package come forward. Schweitzer wanted to see a budget before he would agree to tax breaks. "The one thing that we Democrats in the senate did not expect and were not prepared for and could not fathom was to have a house leadership that was willing to drive off a bridge," Elliott said. "We're not used to having zealots in leadership."

For many in the state, Sales was a surprising choice for the Republicans to elect as speaker. A businessman from Bozeman, his first session was in 2003. He made waves right away when he picked Constitutional Party member Rick Jore, a vocal critic of public education, as chairman of the House Education Committee. Republicans also elected Michael Lange of Billings as majority leader. Lange was clear on his agenda for the session. "My job is to show no quarter to the Democrats as they try to push their liberal agenda," he told Lee reporters Dennison and McKee.

With Sales in the lead, house Republican leaders discarded Schweitzer's proposed budget entirely and instead put forward eight separate budget bills of their own. Taken as a whole, these bills were meant to balance the budget. Typically, however, the budget moves through the legislature as a single bill. This strategy meant the budget arrived at Schweitzer's desk in pieces. Signing or vetoing one bill would affect the others, which were still on the floor being debated.

As the session wore on, the house became the focal point of conflict. In a column printed April 23 in the *Billings Gazette*, Chuck Johnson wrote, "Late last week, House Speaker Scott Sales, R-Bozeman, stunned people by announcing that the House won't even take up the Senate amendments on four major state spending bills until Schweitzer signs a tax relief bill.... The trouble is, the House Republicans' property tax relief bill is a gnarly proposal tied up in school funding, thereby combining two of the densest issues in state government. There doesn't even seem to be a firm proposal in writing at this stage."

The senate managed to maintain its sense of decorum, but the house turned into a circus. Representative Michael Lange, a Republican from Billings, after meeting with the governor and his staff to try and reach a budget compromise, launched into a very public tirade against the governor. Schweitzer had asked Lange to support some of the Democrats' bills, and in return the Democrats and the governor's office would support Lange's tax-relief packages.

Schweitzer felt the meeting was cordial. But Lange had a different take. In front of television cameras and teenage legislative interns, he lost all sense of decorum and control: "My message to the governor is, 'Stick it up your ass!' That's my message to him: 'Stick it up your ass!' I give a crap about honor and dignity and sticking up for what you believe in. Today's the day I'm pissed off at that S.O.B. on the second floor [Schweitzer] that thinks he's going to run the state like a dictator. So I want each and every one of you to get pissed off today because your way of lifestyle is under threat. It isn't about a few million bucks in the budget or a deal for a thousand-dollar bill or any other of that crap. It doesn't mean anything. He can table every bill I have; I don't give a shit!" Lange finished. "I will not be offered a bribe."

Lange's unprofessional rant quickly made its way onto YouTube. com, instantly making the Republican the most infamous legislator of the session. After the tirade he received a brief round of applause from many of the lawmakers present. Some looked shocked. But none, during the meeting, admonished Lange for his outburst.

Weeks later, Schweitzer asked, "How do they explain to their families that they didn't get up and walk out? They would have expected them to do the right thing and they didn't." He seemed more hurt than offended. He later said that some of the Republicans in the room were his friends, and it bothered him that they just let Lange say what he said without a word. It's a scene that will be replayed in the minds of voters during the next elections. They'll want to know why their legislator didn't stand up against such behavior, Schweitzer said.

Lange was asked about his comments immediately following the caucus meeting, and he reiterated that he meant every word. But later in the day he apologized to the house for his comments, calling them "inappropriate." The next day, after news media around the state ran and reran the videotaped tirade, Lange apologized to Schweitzer.

Schweitzer took the high road. "I have the utmost respect for Representative Lange," he said. "One small outburst is certainly not the measure of the man."

When Lange met with Schweitzer and apologized both to him and his wife for the outburst Montana Public Radio was there and recorded the twenty-minute meeting. Schweitzer responded, "Don't worry about it for even a moment. Mike, you know there's no hard feelings and I mean that. I know that you're under a great deal of pressure. . . . I know how difficult it is to be away from your family."

The 2007 legislature adjourned on its last day without passing a budget for the next two years, as is required by the state constitution. The stalemate in the house was largely to blame for the failure. "I just have to shake my head and say this session will be remembered as fifty-one flew over the cuckoo's nest," Schweitzer told the Associated Press on the last day of the session, in reference to the fifty-one Republicans in the house. "This is the theater of the absurd."

After the session Scott Sales blamed the Democrats for being unwilling to compromise. The Republicans were set on giving the budget surplus back to the people of Montana, he said. But they didn't receive any help from the Democrats. In a press conference immediately after the session, he said, "We've met a brick wall at every stage of the way. There was absolutely no compromise with the Democrats. They wanted to spend it all and then some."

Schweitzer was publicly critical of the legislature. During the subsequent special session he was quoted as saying the legislature was "drinking that whiskey and eating thick steaks provided by lobbyists." The statement, while intended to criticize lobbyists (whom Schweitzer clearly dislikes), didn't distinguish between Democrats or Republicans.

A little more than a week after the session, twelve house Republicans met with Schweitzer's staff in a cabin near Helena to hammer out a compromise. These were largely considered the moderate Republicans, although Lange also attended.

Schweitzer, however, wasn't at the meeting. In 2007, he served as fund-raising chairman for the Democratic Governors Association. When the legislators and his staff were meeting in the backcountry cabin, Schweitzer was at the Kentucky Derby for the DGA. It was an event he was obligated to attend. "I didn't spend a lot of time down in the legislature," he said. "I didn't want to have an overbearing presence." At the derby Schweitzer was in cell phone communication with the people at the meeting.

He remains appreciative of the Republicans who attended the meeting, particularly because the session had been so bitterly partisan. They showed true leadership, Schweitzer said. "They knew the other members of their party will come after them in a big way." Once a compromise was struck, Schweitzer called a special session and lawmakers passed a budget and other key bills in five days.

After the special session Lange was voted out as majority leader. But later in 2007 he announced his bid to run against U.S. senator Max Baucus.

Schweitzer says the session demonstrated what the Republicans see as leadership: "The language Mike Lange used in front of that camera is the language that they used among themselves; . . . there just happened to be a camera on them."

In light of Lange's behavior, the Republican claims that Schweitzer is a bully seem rather hollow. "If you're looking for someone who's a bully, I don't think you have to get too far outside the Republican leadership," Schweitzer said.

Not all Republican reactions to Schweitzer have been negative. In 2007 Jim Shockley, a Republican senator from Victor, said that he gets along better with Schweitzer than he has with other governors. "He is the best politician I've seen since I've been in politics, and that includes Racicot."

r has been critical of the role of lobbyists in the legislative
int that's troublesome to both Shockley and Democratic
Elliott. Lobbyists, despite Schweitzer's feelings, play an
e in state politics.

legislators don't have a staff. They are solely responsible
their way through the more than two thousand bills that
e down during the session. Lobbyists help to keep the
formed. Granted, the information they provide is biased,
a vested interest in staying honest. If they aren't, they lose
ibility with lawmakers. "I have to have those people telling
of the story because I can't do it myself," Shockley said. "If
es to me, I'm going to remember it."

er maintains that lobbyists, while necessary, have more
the government than they should. "I didn't say they
weren't necessary; I just said I don't think they're the fourth branch of
government. I don't think they're necessary to buy votes."

In 2007, Schweitzer was again unable to pass his ethics bill that would
have made it against the law for legislators to work as lobbyist for the first
two years after they finished serving. For him, it is a regrettable failure.
However, he's taken a hard stand against lobbyists from the beginning.
He won't appoint a lobbyist to any of the many state commissions
and advisory boards, though previous governors had no problem with
the practice. "These are supposed to be citizen boards and previous
administrations had filled them up about a third with lobbyists. Why
would you select someone who's paid to have a point of view to serve as
a citizen? They're not citizens. They're paid by some corporation to have
a particular point of view."

Lobbyists don't represent the interests of the electorate but rather
those of their employers. Schweitzer has pushed for more transparency in
how much lobbyists spend on legislators during the session. If lobbyists are
going to be part of government, then they need to be more forthcoming
about how they influence legislation, he said. "I'm the least popular

governor in the history of this state with lobbyists." And he's proud of that. "You're not going to buy your way to the front of the line."

But it's been argued that painting all lobbyists with such a broad brush is inaccurate. While there are lobbyists for oil, realtors, and big business, there are also lobbyists for children's health care, education, and environmental concerns. "If we didn't have lobbyists, we'd be even less sophisticated than we are. It's our only chance to gather information," Shockley said.

27

The Man with the Plan

The Governor's Mansion in Helena is a curious building. Built in 1959, it's situated two blocks from the Capitol in a quiet middle-class neighborhood. While other states tend to prefer more stately, traditional mansions for the governor, Montana sports a faux-moderne split-level, rather reminiscent of butterfly collars and disco balls, kind of like Steve Austin meets Hugh Hefner.

If Schweitzer were to pursue national office, he'd certainly have better digs, but he's consistently maintained that he doesn't have any desire for public office greater than the governor of Montana, which, he says, is the greatest job in the world. When I asked him about the possibility of being tapped to run as vice president and getting a room in the White House, he flippantly said: "I heard those rooms go for about $5,000 a night. I don't have that kind of money."

Few journalists have covered Schweitzer more than Chuck Johnson, and even Johnson hasn't seen or heard indication that Schweitzer plans to run for higher office. Still the rumors persist. How could someone with as much political talent as Schweitzer just ride off into the sunset after eight years in office? And if he doesn't have national ambition, what's a governor from a state with less than a million people doing suggesting energy policy to the nation? Since taking office he's appeared at least twice before the U.S. Congress, he's been interviewed by *60 Minutes*, CNN, and Charlie Rose, and he's sat across from Bill Maher on HBO's *Real Time*. He has garnered more press attention than any other Montana governor in history. It's not even close.

Schweitzer entered the governor's office in Helena during a time of change, nationally, for the Democratic Party. Democrats have traditionally looked to the South for their battleground states. The feeling has been that if they could beat or match Republicans during a presidential race in the South, then they had a good chance of winning the oval office. In the last two presidential elections, however, Democrats lost the Bible Belt wholesale and yet still came very close to beating George W. Bush. And some argue, of course, that they did beat him.

New battleground states are going to be in the Rocky Mountain West, Charles Mahtesian said. Those states could be Colorado and Arizona, and possibly Montana. Democrats here have given the national party a road map for success. "Schweitzer isn't just a leader in the changes happening out here," Mahtesian said. "I think of him as *the* leader. He's the darling of the national party."

Clearly, Schweitzer's primary focus, the one that's gained him the most attention, is energy. Given his master's degree in soil science from Montana State University in 1980, he's been uniquely positioned to push his ambitious coal-into-diesel scenario. He sees it as a salvation not just for Montana but also for the nation. And he sells it with the fervency of a tent revivalist, calling for an end to America's addiction to foreign oil and labeling the leaders of most Middle Eastern countries "sheiks, rats, and dictators."

It's proven a formula too tempting to resist: the cowboy governor from an outback state, pushing a scenario that could potentially rescue the country from its dependence on foreign oil. He's been teased on the

Colbert Report (Colbert pointed to him and said, "Okay, bolo, you want to go bolo tie; that's your style." And then quickly slipping on his own bolo tie, "There it is," Colbert said. "I feel like I can go rope a steer."). He presented himself as solemn and professional with the National Press Club (he began his speech by saying, "I'd like to talk to you today about something that's probably more important than anything that's touched this country in generations, and that's the inability to produce our own energy."). He flirted with Leslie Stahl on *60 Minutes* and came across as stern and resolute with Charlie Rose. He's spoken with the Senate Finance Committee, toured the war zones in the Middle East with Mitt Romney, and written columns for the *New York Times,* all mostly in the interests of bringing coal-into-diesel interests to Montana.

The resistance he's met in this regard (an article in the *Denver Post,* dated November 1, 2007, claimed that "at least 10 proposals for coal-gasification plants in the U.S. have been delayed or canceled this year. The plans have succumbed to high costs, technological uncertainties, and growing concern about carbon emissions from coal-fired power") should not reflect on the good intentions of his ambition. The technology, politics and policy perhaps haven't caught up to him yet. As a foundation for his plan, Schweitzer points to his experience in the Middle East, his education as a soil scientist, and his history as a businessman. He will tell you he knows all about America's dependence on foreign oil, and he knows how to break it. He's not a one-issue politician, but his other issues are Montana centric. His energy plan is global. In a nutshell it stands on three legs: conservation, clean and green energy, and clean coal.

According to Schweitzer, America uses well over 6.5 billion barrels of oil a year, of which 4.5 billion are imported, mainly from the Middle East and Central and South America. With smart conservation, such as more-efficient cars and less driving, Americans could cut consumption by at least a billion barrels of oil a year.

With regard to biofuels Schweitzer maintains that if we used all the acreage in America that is planted with crops exported out of country, we could produce a billion barrels of biofuel. The key would lie in not reducing food supply. The crops planted for biofuel would need to be on those acres currently not in use for domestic food production.

But the lynchpin of his plan relates to clean coal.

In 1923 German scientists developed a process for generating diesel from coal. This Fischer-Tropsch process supplied the embargoed Nazis and Japanese in World War II. Later it fueled apartheid South Africa. "What you do first is the coal gasification process," Schweitzer told Chuck Johnson in a newspaper article. "You crush the coal up, heat it and get your gas. From there, it's a chemical reaction. You have a big tank and use either cobalt or iron as the catalyst. What you get out of that is the building blocks to make fuel. You get carbon monoxide and you get hydrogen. With those two you can make any fuel you would like to make—diesel, gasoline, heating fuel, plastics, fertilizer or pure hydrogen."

The process, however, creates a significant amount of carbon dioxide, the leading greenhouse gas. Schweitzer promised Leslie Stahl that he would not let that gas into the atmosphere. Instead, coal-to-fuel plants would either sequester the carbon dioxide in underground geologic formations or pump it to an oil well and let them use it to pressure the last drops of crude oil out of the ground.

America has a third of the world's coal reserves, Schweitzer said. And Montana has a third of the nation's coal. And while he understands that people have problems with coal and how it's traditionally been used, if the emerging technology was used to treat the coal in an environmentally friendly way (sequestering the carbon dioxide underground), we could produce more than two billion barrels of relatively clean fuel a year.

The principal issue is sequestration. It's very much an emerging science. What would happen if the carbon dioxide escaped into an underground aquifer or leaked back to the surface? The unintended consequences are still unknown. However, Schweitzer is quick to point out that carbon dioxide, in some cases, exists naturally in underground seems. And oil drillers have been using it for years to help push oil out of the ground. It's a process called enhanced oil recovery, Schweitzer said. They simply pump carbon dioxide back into the ground and the gas displaces the oil from the oil formations and allows it to be pumped to the surface. However, as of now, there's no economic or regulatory framework established to oversee a massive carbon sequestration process. (Sequestration would also require a federal investment of at least $10 billion in research to find the geological structures available to receive the carbon dioxide.) The technology is there to sequester carbon dioxide safely, Schweitzer said, but the disincentives aren't in place yet to keep coal plants from continuing to pump carbon dioxide into the atmosphere. They aren't in place because Congress hasn't acted. "Really until Congress creates the rules regarding clean coal technology, there'll be no change. People know the change is coming but Congress hasn't acted."

To his mind, the biggest problem with sequestering carbon dioxide is cost. "It's going to cost at least thirty dollars per ton of carbon dioxide to sequester it. There are two tons of carbon dioxide produced for every ton of coal that you started with." This costs has continued to tip the balance toward other types of energy. "What it does is for some public policy makers—it says to them 'I better hold back on this because I have some supporters in the coal industry who aren't going to like this.'"

In an August 2007 *Missoula Independent* article, journalist John Adams opined that the roadblock to sequestration is Congress's reluctance to regulate and tax carbon emissions. "Currently there are no restrictions on CO_2 emissions, but most observers seem to agree that in the coming years lawmakers . . . will have to create disincentives for dumping greenhouse gases into the air. . . . That means old, dirty coal-fired power plants are likely to become much more expensive as carbon emissions become taxed. Until that happens, investors aren't lining up to spend their own money on unproven technologies to remove and sequester carbon."

Another hurdle is funding. So far no companies have put money behind a significant coal-to-liquids (CTL) plant in Montana. One plant, as announced by Schweitzer in October of 2006, was apparently planned near the town of Roundup in eastern Montana. Schweitzer said it would produce twenty-two thousand barrels of synfuel a day and three hundred megawatts of electricity, even while containing the carbon dioxide emissions. He was quick to say that the deal was a private endeavor between energy development corporations.

But the plant hit speed bumps in 2007. The air-quality permit, which was originally approved for a standard coal-fired power plant, expired, and attempts to modify it for a coal-to-liquids plant were denied by the Montana Department of Environmental Quality. Furthermore, in September of 2007, John Adams of the *Missoula Independent* found that the companies identified as partnering in the plant's development were telling another story. "Arch Coal of St. Louis is the second-largest coal producer in the country and a 25-percent partner with DKRW Advanced Fuels, the company named by the governor's office as the 'primary developer' of the CTL project. When contacted by the *Independent* earlier this week, both Arch Coal and DKRW denied involvement with the Roundup CTL plant."

Schweitzer said Montana wasn't involved in the Bull Mountain project, as an investor or a promoter. The companies involved issued a press release and Schweitzer simply commented on it. "That's the way those things go, it's not something we conjured up."

The crux of the matter is that Bull Mountain Coal lost its claim to the coal, he said. "So if you're the other two partners and one of your partners steps back from the table and says 'Boys I'm out of the game, I'm out of chips' then you need to move on with another proposition. And I think that's what happened in that case." While the Bull Mountain project remains in limbo, Schweitzer may have found another option with the military. In October of 2007 the U.S. Air Force announced plans to explore building a CTL plant on the Malmstrom base near Great Falls. The air force has said it's dedicated to changing its planes from regular jet fuel to the synfuel produced in the CTL process.

The hurdles haven't stopped Schweitzer or even slowed him down. He's still pushing his plan and possibly wagering his political future on it. And though clean coal might not be a perfect solution, it is indeed a possible way for America to twelve-step itself away from foreign-oil addiction. "Forty, fifty years from now we'll be in a new economy when it comes to energy," Schweitzer has said. "We need planks on the bridge to the future. Either we continue to enrich those dictators by sending $240 billion a year to their economies or we produce those bridge fuels domestically."

However, the fact remains that any of these CTL projects will take years to develop. The approval process takes about five years, Schweitzer told me. The technology to sequester the carbon dioxide is new, and many of the planned CTL plants are going back to the drawing boards to rework their plans.

Schweitzer said, "With or without Brian Schweitzer, these projects are going to be built. We have an insatiable demand for energy. I'm just trying to be part of change and not just riding the bus of change."

But until clean coal becomes more of a reality, Schweitzer said he is going to continue to support other aspects of clean and green energy, like wind and solar power. "I'm agnostic as to which of those clean green energy sources we use."

This is part of the reason why Schweitzer joined Montana into the Western Climate Initiative in November 2007. The WCI includes California, Oregon, New Mexico, Arizona, Washington, Utah, British Columbia, and Manitoba. "We have agreed that we will decrease our carbon footprint substantially. And we have agreed that we will find ways of producing and consuming energy all the while decreasing our carbon foot print."

Along with this energy plan comes a policy for the Middle East. Schweitzer disagrees with the war—"I never thought the Iraqi venture was worth a damn"—and is maybe the first Montana governor with a background such that his opinions carry weight outside of the state.

Having lived there, Schweitzer knows more about the Middle East than probably any other governor in the country. It's his opinion that to try to force democracy on a region that has long been ruled by religious radicals is useless.

He told Charlie Rose, "I'm going to say something that people aren't going to like to hear. They say how soon are we going to get out of Iraq? When are we leaving? We're not. In fact we're going to have more than one hundred thousand of our men and women in the Middle East as long as we're importing oil."

Schweitzer calls it serendipitous that he came into office when he did. As a point, he refers to his unusual resume. "That group of experiences [in the Middle East] coupled with my scientific curiosity led me forward; and ultimately when I'm about fifty years old, I become governor of one of the largest potential energy producers in the United States at a time where we have sent hundreds of thousands of men and women to the Middle East to secure oil supplies for dictators and others."

"So I'm able to put all of those pieces together and as I cobble those pieces together it creates a picture to me that is crystal clear. That our greatest challenge is to create new energy systems in the country, in both the way we consume and the way we produce, so that we're able to produce a clean, green domestic energy system, so that we no longer will be reliant on foreign dictators. That we will no longer have to send both the blood of our young people and the treasure from our coffers to defend their energy systems." For someone with such strong opinions about national policy, it must be frustrating to be on the figurative sidelines, limited to the corral of your own rural state.

He's the governor of Montana. Is he satisfied with that? He scoffs at the idea of national office but clearly has larger designs. "Being in this place at this time and I think with a laser-light focus on what I believe to be, and I think many are beginning to agree with me, the greatest challenge, not only to this generation, but the greatest challenge of the generations that have come before us and all of the generations that will follow us will be faced with. It's now and we have the opportunity. With that comes the challenge to get it right. That's a passion that drives me day and night.

"I'm trying to change the world now. If we can change the way we consume and produce energy in this country, if we can become self-sufficient without increasing carbon dioxide, if we can produce clean and green energy technology in this country that we can export to the entire world, I could walk away from this and never come back."

28

Montana's National Politics

The dedication ceremony was simple but profound. A crowd of about one hundred friends and family gathered on a bridge across Rock Creek, near Philipsburg. The summer heat cooked the asphalt, and those in ties and dress shirts were sweating. The wind blew dust off the road and into our faces.

Brian Schweitzer stood with the family of Pfc. Kyle G. Bohrnsen, twenty-two, of Philipsburg. He had died on April 10, 2007, in Baghdad, when his vehicle had hit an improvised explosive device. The bridge, located on Montana Highway 348, now bears Kyle's name.

"Kyle loved this spot," Schweitzer told the group as he looked up the pastoral Rock Creek valley. He went on to talk about the spirit of Bohrnsen and how it would live on in us and how his and his family's sacrifice would never be forgotten. Kyle's parents spoke about their love for their son. When his mother broke down, Schweitzer put a hand on her shoulder, his face grave. On such a sunny, clear day, the dark emotions made for a stark contrast. After the ceremony Schweitzer and Jag posed for pictures with the family.

Montana has the highest military service rate in America, with about 8.5 enlistees for every 10,000 citizens. As a result many families around the state find themselves dealing with the loss of a child, parent, or spouse who won't be coming home from Iraq. The bridge dedication was one of several similar events Schweitzer has attended since taking office. It's something that clearly wears on him. When he talks about the war, about Montana losing its soldiers, he is regretful, outraged. On the *Today Show* he said, "We, we're faced with funerals. What do you say to the families? If somebody could give me a script, I would like it because this is the most difficult part of my job is . . . to try and make sense of all this. Everyone's asking when does it end? How does it end?"

Regardless of the reasons or rationale behind the war, Montanans are there. Not long ago, Schweitzer showed me an e-mail from a mother whose son was killed in Iraq. He had attended the funeral and the mother was thanking him. "It was not the military that picked this war," Schweitzer said staring at a printout of the e-mail. "The civilian leaders decided when we go to war. . . . The system didn't work this time."

But families don't want to hear this, so Schweitzer navigates those conversations with more delicacy. "This is very difficult for you. This is very difficult for me," he'll say. "Any time next month, next year call me. Call me at home. If you're having trouble coping, call me anytime."

29

The Family

Arguably, Schweitzer's biggest job is being a father. It's not something that gets talked about in the media much—he tries to keep his three kids removed from the public eye—but he is devoted to his family. Middle son, Khai, is enrolled in Montana Tech in Butte, studying engineering. Katrina is a senior in high school. His oldest son, Ben, is autistic and lives at home.

"More than anything else being a parent humbles you," Schweitzer said. "It demonstrates that you're not in control of anything. You have aspirations for your children and hope that they'll do things bigger and better than you did. However, for all the wishing and praying, they have to live their own lives."

Being the father of a special-needs child is even more humbling. Ben has Asperger's syndrome. He struggles with social and organizational skills, Schweitzer said, but is intelligent and enthusiastic. "He has to find his way in this world and he's been given a bigger cross to bear than a lot of us have."

With Ben, Schweitzer has different expectations. "The most important and humbling thing to know is they're not going to be the leader in industry or the mover and shaker in politics or the scientist that changes the world. I want my child to be happy and I want him to be able to live on his own sometime in his life." Ben's challenges are great, but his enthusiasm is inspiring, Schweitzer said.

When your dad is the governor, life isn't always that easy. "That's probably an extra burden for my kids, and they didn't ask for it, and I guess I never thought about it when I got into this business," he said. "I suppose it's character building."

But not all of it builds character. Schweitzer talked about a particular instance that involved Ben when he was attending Whitefish High School during Schweitzer's campaign for governor. Ben has difficulty taking tests, so his teachers would work with a special education assistant who would give Ben tests orally. Sometimes Ben loses his homework, too. The assistant would keep in touch with Ben's other teachers to make sure he was keeping up with assignments. This was often done through e-mail communication. But one of Ben's teachers, a Bob Brown supporter, apparently forwarded a string of private e-mails discussing Ben's work and progress. He also wrote a note: "And this kid's dad wants to be governor."

Even now, three years later, Schweitzer is still incensed. His voice rises as he says, "A guy who's supposed to be a teacher, a career involving children ... who would do such a thing as violate all of the privacy for this kid? A kid who before he was ten years old had more challenges than that son of a bitch, that teacher ... than he'll have his entire life, and this guy for pure partisan politics attempted to, I don't know what he was attempting to do, but I was outraged."

For Ben it was tough. He trusted the adults who were caring for him, and this one teacher's actions violated that trust. But it was probably tougher for the rest of the family. "We are his protectors and I view myself as his protector and I will be for the rest of my life," Schweitzer said.

People can say what they want about him personally, he added, but turning your political ire toward someone's kids is another thing. "Those that attack people's families, those who try to use children in politics, I think there's a special place in hell for them to burn."

Schweitzer does what he can to protect his kids and family from the weight of his office. But they still read the newspaper, they still read what people are saying about him, and that's tough, particularly on Nancy, he said.

"Nancy's got a little thinner skin than I do, and she reads the paper, and she's says, 'How can they possibly say that? None of that's true. Why would they say such a thing?' I kind of shrug my shoulders and attempt to set the record straight and say something nice about the people who said something terrible about me."

30

From Around Here

Walk into Charlie B's bar in Missoula on any given summer night, and you'll soon find yourself sitting on a stool with a rancher on one side and a smoke jumper on the other. Chances are they know each other, maybe worked together on a slash crew back in college. They're part of the community. They trust each other. Despite all the recent growth, Montana still has very much a small-town atmosphere.

Brian Schweitzer grew up on a ranch. He was reared in the midst of people who scraped their living off the land. He knows what it means for people to trust you. When he ran ads, he didn't try to look like a politician; he looked like himself, shooting guns with his son, riding horses, talking about health care, about balancing the budget.

Under the style, though—and as a product of his environment—well . . . It's perhaps a reflection of the state of national politics that when a politician is a regular guy, he makes news. The vast majority of Montanans own guns, like dogs, appreciate Native American heritage, and are known to have a shot of whiskey now and then.

Most of Montana's high-profile politicians have come from a blue-collar background. Democrat Mike Mansfield rose to the U.S. Senate and an ambassadorship to Japan, but he got his start slugging away in the mines of Butte. Republican Marc Racicot was born in the small mining town of Libby. Schweitzer is constantly thumping the fact that he's just a rancher. "Look, these are ideas that anybody could come up with if they had the time to think about it," he said. "I'm going to stand up and fight for the little guy every single time."

He thinks everyone ought to have a shot at an education and health care. He's still promoting cheaper prescription drugs, and during both his bid for governor in 2004 and his Senate campaign in 2000, he ran ads that showed him with gun in hand. When the Bush administration proposed restructuring the Farm Service Agency and closing down offices in several small towns around Montana, Schweitzer fought back. When Bush wanted to sell off pieces of national forest, Schweitzer equated Bush to a rancher who spends money on a new truck and combine but then has to sell off his back forty. When Bush was sending National Guard troops to Iraq, Schweitzer was demanding (fruitlessly, as it turned out) for them to come home and help fight wildfires. But if you press him for an answer as to why he's developed some of his positions, he answers enigmatically. "Politics is complicated stuff," he says. "Who the heck can figure this stuff out?"

31

Us and Them

Schweitzer has said that he has thick skin, but he also keeps a close eye on his opponents. The first time I met with him in his office at the Capitol, he told me he checks newspapers every morning to see what people are saying about him. During our interview he went to his computer to Google his own name in the online media.

During his gubernatorial race in 2004, bipartisanship was a conspicuous leg of Brian Schweitzer's platform. "Someone that can say something nice to their political rivals, I think that's still a value." Putting small business before big business, providing better education and health care for all Montanans, these ideas, he said, shouldn't be partisan.

But this commitment to bipartisanship doesn't mean he's never tough on the other party. In a speech to a room of land-use planners, I once saw him present a graph showing energy development in Montana over the past thirty or so years. The graph depicted how under Republican governors, energy development was stagnant. But under Democratic governors, meaning him and Schwinden, energy production increased. Typical for Schweitzer, the graph pointed out two things: first, his own successes, and second, the failures of his Republican counterparts.

He thrives in the face of adversity. He's scrappy and needs an opponent. In the summer of 2007, I spoke to him on the telephone just after he'd given a speech to a Montana Chamber of Commerce meeting. He wasn't happy.

"The Montana Chamber," he replied, "they spend all their time telling the world that we have a bad place to do business. . . . The reason they don't like the economy of Montana is because the governor's a Democrat. . . . It's actually outrageous that I'm faced with people who are supposed to represent business interests, and they spend all their time bad-mouthing Montana's business."

Brian Schweitzer has taken pains to avoid characterizing himself as a die-hard Democrat. "What I say is, I'm not beholden to any political party. Sometimes the Republicans get it right and sometimes the Democrats get it right." During the 2006 election, however, Schweitzer sent postcards to voters endorsing Democratic candidates. In some districts, in fact, Schweitzer sent out several rounds of campaign literature. In his day-to-day running of the state, Schweitzer is so passionate about his own agenda that he continues to be critical of those who disagree with him, and his ire tends to fall along party lines. He occasionally uses his place in the spotlight to disparage those groups who haven't supported him or the legislators who disagree with him.

He almost certainly stepped on his own toes during a 2006 interaction with the Montana Stockgrowers. The oldest cattlemen's group in the state, the Stockgrowers Association is, by and large, a conservative group. Although the group is officially nonpartisan, they are largely conservative and Schweitzer has characterized them, using familiar language, as "the Republican wing of the Republican party."

The Stockgrowers' president in 2006 was Bill Donald, a rancher from Melville, Montana. He and Schweitzer didn't get along. "[Donald] thought his job was to say anything disparaging he could about the Democratic governor," Schweitzer said. And Donald also classified their relationship as rocky. "Despite his efforts to portray himself as bipartisan, he was probably one of the more partisan politicians I've ever worked with. We tried to work through that, but with limited success I would say."

In 2006, knowing the Stockgrowers had problems with his ideas for bison management around Yellowstone, Schweitzer invited Donald and other Stockgrowers members to the governor's mansion for a meeting. According to Donald, the meeting didn't go well. "It wasn't so much a visit as getting lectured to for two hours," he said.

Schweitzer sees things differently. "I had them into my home and spent time with them and thought we had a great meeting," he said. "Come to find out, [Donald] didn't get two blocks away before he was on his cell phone calling people and telling them things happened that didn't happen, telling them we said things we didn't say, and telling them we didn't have a good meeting here."

Bison management north of Yellowstone National Park has long been a politically divisive issue. The buffalo and elk within the park often carry brucellosis, a disease that can cause cows to abort their calves. Though some of the science is inconclusive, having park buffalo mingle with domestic cattle could potentially threaten the cattle with infection. (A brucellosis-free certification for a cattle herd also means greater profitability in the market.) To avoid the intermingling of buffalo and cattle, Montana has taken a number of different measures, including hazing, hunting, and culling. Part of Schweitzer's solution included pulling back some of the cattle that graze on the boundary of the park, creating a buffer zone. The Stockgrowers, however, were uncomfortable giving up ground to bison.

By his own admittance Schweitzer isn't a typical politician. "I was never the favorite of the Democratic Party when I got started in this business, and I probably won't be when I'm done," he said. "I'm not a traditional kind of person, and I will stretch the bounds of what people think are their orthodox positions."

Schweitzer continued to disagree with the Stockgrowers over bison management. The debate was further complicated when a cattle herd north of Yellowstone National Park tested positive for brucellosis in the spring of 2007. The rancher who owned the herd was forced to slaughter six hundred head of cattle. Montana was on the verge of losing its brucellosis-free status. (Another positive test within two years of the first and Montana will indeed lose its status.)

Schweitzer pushed for a split-state scenario in dealing with brucellosis. It seemed like a commonsense solution. One "state" would be around Yellowstone; the other state would be the rest of Montana. The federal government agreed to consider the idea, but it needed to pass muster with the Montana Department of Livestock and their seven-member board.

The issue became very political. The Stockgrowers Association was against the idea, saying it would unfairly harm a handful of ranchers. The Montana Cattlemen's Association, the state's Democrat-leaning cattle group, backed Schweitzer's plan.

The struggles with the Stockgrowers Association is frustrating for Schweitzer, particularly because he's a rancher and feels like he knows as much as any politician about good policies for the agriculture community in Montana. "People will bring a partisan-biased opinion to an issue and then they will attempt to craft their opinion around their bias." Schweitzer's stance on how to try and manage brucellosis was based on science and what was good for Montana. It was a position he was uniquely qualified to make.

"I arguably know as much about cattle, bison, and this disease . . . as anybody who's involved in the debate or maybe more. I've actually made my living in exporting semen and frozen embryos and live cattle all over the world," Schweitzer said. Other countries that import American beef, whether it is live cattle, semen or embryos, want to know that it comes from a place that is free of disease. "If we're not considered free of some of these critical diseases, those people in the export business are out of business. I entered this debate attempting to do the right thing by the cattle industry, the wildlife industry. I approach it in a manner that is based on science, not on emotion."

In November 2007 the Montana Livestock Board voted six to one against the split-state idea. Though Schweitzer was disappointed, he didn't hold the Stockgrowers Association in contempt. "I've proposed many, many policies and laws that are good for Montana cattlemen and Montana farm families. I hold no animosity toward any individual or any group."

32

The Sportsman

A key and divisive part of the West's growth has been an influx of what locals refer to as "out-of-staters." The way some people say it, the term has near racist overtones. As the economy and culture segue from agriculture to development and recreation, as the rivers and ski hills grow more crowded, as communities become diluted with immigrants who may or may not have an investment in the infrastructure, residency has come to take on certain overtones of legitimacy.

For a number of sportsmen, the influx of out-of-staters has meant, most of all, a flowering of No Trespassing signs. And while many of the new landowners might be willing to allow hunting and limited access, the uproar by locals against them leaves them feeling ostracized and alienated. Few issues have focused the attentions of these disparate communities so much as Montana's stream-access law. In 1985 the state legislature said that the bed and banks of a natural stream, up to the high-water mark, are public land and as such available for recreational access. The most liberal stream-access law in the country, it has been upheld twice by the Montana Supreme Court. But cases still arise where sportsmen and landowners clash on the interpretation of the law.

Schweitzer's campaign recognized the importance of appealing to Montana's sporting community. According to the U.S. Fish and Wildlife Service, nearly five hundred thousand of the state's residents hunt and fish. They spend about $550 million a year on gear, travel, and licenses. Schweitzer and his campaign ran ads showing him walking through the woods with his brother Walter, clad in hunter orange and camo, holding a rifle.

Author David Sirota works for the Center for American Progress but took a leave of absence to work on Schweitzer's campaign. In a revealing and artful article for *Washington Monthly,* he discussed how Schweitzer courted the support of sportsmen in Montana and pushed to communicate his allegiance with them throughout his campaign for governor:

> As I was wolfing down a bowl of cereal at my desk in Whitefish this past October, my cell phone rang. It was Schweitzer. Since he's usually up by 4 a.m., and buzzing off two pots of coffee by 6, it was always a bad sign to get a call from him before dawn.
>
> "When's the gun ad going up?" he demanded to know without a hello, the caffeine making his voice quiver ever so slightly. He was calling from the side of a rural highway where his single-engine plane had been forced to land because of bad weather. But all he wanted to talk about was the gun ad.
>
> "Ahh... I can check with —"
>
> "Listen to me very carefully, and get your head in the game," he said, voice rising. "No matter what our major ad of the week is, I want that damn gun ad running under everything! I want it in every media market, and I want it on TV and radio. The next time I call, I want to know it's happening."

The sporting community is a demographic Schweitzer can relate to. He himself is a hunter and fisherman. He received an A-minus from the National Rifle Association (his gubernatorial opponent in 2004, Bob Brown, received an A) and made it a point in his campaign to tout Montana's access laws. If he could portray himself as sharing the same concerns and goals—land access, gun rights, conservation—then he felt he could make inroads with them.

But it's a difficult and divisive thing, walking the tightrope between populist concerns of public access and the rights of private landowners, some of whom are the wealthiest residents of the state. If you're a politician, being able to bounce back and forth between these polarized players in such a way as to keep from alienating everyone is a magic trick that David Copperfield might envy. A public access issue in Ravalli County is particularly telling.

The Mitchell Slough is a fairly insignificant waterway that starts and ends on the Bitterroot River. The whole length of the slough is on private land. It's only twelve miles long but runs through some of the last large pieces of open space in the Bitterroot Valley. Some of the landowners on the slough include investment mogul Charles Schwab, musician Huey Lewis, investor Ken Seibel, and Las Vegas developer Anthony Marnell. Other landowners are notable for their legacy rather than their wealth or fame. Bill Strange, for instance, works land his family has farmed for generations. In any case, no matter their divergent backgrounds, every landowner along the slough says it's a private ditch dug in the late 1860s and early 1870s. For some local sportsmen, though, the slough is very significant. They see it as a public waterway that landowners are wrongly attempting to make private.

Ken Seibel bought his land on the slough in 1979. He was told it was a private ditch and went to work changing the waterway from a wide, slow, muddy slough into a sinuous streamlike watercourse. His work was mimicked by other wealthy landowners, and within a few years, the slough was home to an amazing trout fishery. Landowners say this work made the Mitchell Slough into the fishery it is. Sportsmen say it always was amazing trout water. The history of the Mitchell Slough is murky. Court documents and testimony detail evidence back to the mid- to late 1800s, when Ravalli County was first settled by homesteaders. Bill Strange can point to his great-grandfather's journal, which detailed the building of the Mitchell. The other side points to an 1872 General Land Office map that describes the Mitchell as a side channel of the Bitterroot River. As far as fishing goes, everybody agrees that people fished the Mitchell for as long as they remember. The two sides disagree about just how good the fishing was. However, before the passing of Montana's Stream Access law, everyone was expected to ask for permission.

In 1992 two local fishermen, Robert and Randy Rose, decided to test the stream-access law on Mitchell Slough. They called up the state game warden and the local newspaper and told them of their plans to fish the slough on Huey Lewis's land. The editor of a small local newspaper was there and watched as the game warden wrote them a trespassing ticket.

The Rose brothers took the state to court, and a Montana Fish Wildlife and Parks biologist from Missoula told the court that the Mitchell was a public waterway. The trespassing case was thrown out, and the controversy began.

Eventually, through a series of challenges as to origin and nature of the slough, the case ended up in district court in Ravalli County in 2005. The local conservation district board had two years previously determined it was a ditch. A local sportsmen's group was appealing the decision and also asking for a ruling on whether or not the slough was open for public fishing.

The newspaperman that showed up for the Rose brothers' stunt was Michael Howell, who owns the *Bitterroot Star*, a small newspaper in Stevensville. Over the past fifteen years, Howell has decried the landowners on the Mitchell Slough as wealthy out-of-staters who shut the public off from its right to hunt and fish the slough. He even formed an activist group to fight the landowners, the Bitterroot River Protection Association.

The issue couldn't be more complex. It reflects profound social and economic changes as well as the more specific concerns regarding access.

The case has become a rallying point for sportsmen around the state. The Montana Wildlife Federation has supported the BRPA in its fight, as has Montana Trout Unlimited.

The case has also become significant for ranchers and farmers in the state. The Montana Farm Bureau intervened in the case and the Montana Stockgrowers Association has filed a brief in support of the landowners as well.

Initially, when the conservation district determined the slough was a private ditch, then governor Judy Martz prohibited the Montana Fish, Wildlife, and Parks from appealing its decision. Her thought was the conservation district was a state-funded board, and it didn't make sense to pit taxpayers' dollars against each other. The FWP presence in the case was key, because the BRPA, which had appealed the conservation district's decision, didn't have the funds to adequately wage an appeal. Schweitzer was elected to office before the appeal was heard, and he reversed Martz's decision to keep FWP out of the case in January of 2005. It then joined the BRPA in the appeal.

Huey Lewis asked the governor to come visit the slough and listen to the landowners. He also asked the governor to visit with the BRPA and hear their side of the story. Lewis figured if the governor heard both sides and saw the slough for himself, he'd see through the politics of the case.

Lewis and the other landowners on the ditch maintain that the science involved in the case should determine the outcome. The Mitchell Slough is made up of water diverted from the Bitterroot River. This water is blocked, lifted, and pushed east of the river by a series of dams, weirs, and trenches. It serves as both a conveyance ditch for irrigation water and a drainage ditch for irrigation water that has been flooded over farmland and is making its way back to the river.

Bill Strange remembers fishing on the Mitchell, but if he went somewhere off his property he had to ask permission, and he expects people to ask him to fish the stretch of the slough he owns. Before the changes to the Mitchell, it wasn't all that great of a place to fish, especially by the middle of summer, he told me back in the spring of 2005. "The moss would get so thick and the water got real warm."

However, Strange isn't the only longtime Bitterrooter with recollections of the Mitchell. Floyd Wood, whose family came to the valley the same time as Strange's, remembers fishing the Mitchell frequently. "Any claim that the slough is a ditch is ridiculous," Wood told the Montana Wildlife Federation in a history the group wrote about the controversy.

Similarly, the BRPA says the slough is and was a natural side channel of the Bitterroot. Just because farmers have long manipulated its course doesn't mean it's not subject to public access.

Schweitzer came down and met with landowners and sportsmen alike. He saw the slough and looked at it as both a politician and an irrigation specialist. He talked with the farmers about how the water was lifted and pushed. He sympathized with them when they complained about sportsmen who had trespassed on their land. He understood, he said, because he also was a rancher and had to deal with trespassing sportsmen. He also agreed with the sportsmen on the importance of public access. He sympathized with their position. With both groups he initially avoided taking a public stance.

The district court eventually sided with the landowners. Lewis immediately called Schweitzer hoping to convince him not to allow the state to appeal. Schweitzer told Lewis he wanted the landowners to work with local groups to find a solution. According to Lewis, Schweitzer told him: "I need a victory here. . . . If we can find a hundred or two hundred yards that we can allow the public to access that would be good enough."

Lewis says he told Schweitzer he understood completely and said he could put together a coalition of landowners, sportsmen, and conservation groups and turn the focus of the controversy from the contentious battle of access to conserving and protecting the resource and also find places to allow the public to access. According to Lewis, Schweitzer told him he was right on. Schweitzer also gave him the impression that there wouldn't be an appeal: "Yeah, well, it's over because I say enough lawyerin' already," Lewis remembers Schweitzer saying.

About a week later, however, the *New York Times* ran an article on the Mitchell Slough controversy. In it there was no sign of Schweitzer, the conciliator. He had chosen sides. "This decision had to be appealed because it affects streams, creeks, and sloughs all over Montana. It's a natural body of water, and by my reading of the stream access law it should be open to the public to fish and recreate," Schweitzer told reporter, Jim Robbins.

Lewis said the sportsmen groups, the *Bitterroot Star,* and now Schweitzer have done a masterful job of couching the fight of access in the terms of class warfare. "Who doesn't not like rich out-of-staters?" Lewis asks. But Lewis is a resident and feels like he's a good Montanan, a good neighbor. "To paint me as some pig who's trying to fence the public off of historically private ground is just not fair."

Schweitzer still considers Lewis a friend and appreciates his feelings on the Mitchell Slough. But, as governor, he has to consider what's best for Montana, not what's best for his friend. "I was shown the slough through the eyes of Huey Lewis and he was a proponent of a position that I ultimately didn't come down on."

Schweitzer has maintained that he never told Lewis he wasn't going to allow the appeal. He did tell Lewis that he wanted the local landowners and sportsmen to figure out a solution without the courts, but he didn't see that happening and allowed the state to move forward with appealing the district court decision to the Supreme Court. "This decision affects nearly every river in Montana. This case needs to have more clarity."

Schweitzer also said he's focused on the access issue and making sure Montana continues to stand out for the ability of sportsmen to access land to hunt and fish.

"I will protect the right of sportsmen because that's what makes Montana different, the ability to have access to hunting and fishing."

He's also made it clear in the *New York Times* piece that he's not keen on wealthy out-of-staters coming in and shutting off access. "If you want to buy a big ranch and you want to have a river and you want privacy, don't buy in Montana. The rivers belong to the people of Montana," Schweitzer said.

Essentially, Schweitzer knows he's going to make some people unhappy by backing the state's appeal of the district court's decision concerning the Mitchell Slough, but he believes it's the right thing to do for the Bitterroot Valley and, more importantly, Montana. He's an irrigation specialist. He'll admit there's not many things he's an expert at, but irrigation is his forte. And though some disagree with his position concerning the slough, he believes that allowing the state to appeal was the right choice. "It was based on what I know to be the facts in this case and applied Montana law. I can't do more or less."

His stance on the Mitchell Slough has endeared him to the sporting groups in Montana. Craig Sharpe, the executive director of the Montana Wildlife Federation, says Schweitzer's ability to identify with sportsmen has been crucial, because the state is changing and recreation has become a key aspect of the state's economy. "I believe that he recognizes the value to the culture and the economy of Montana of hunters and anglers," Sharpe said.

Republican senator Jim Shockley, from Ravalli County, has also pointed to Schweitzer's stand on the Mitchell Slough as a positive thing. "He helped us on the Mitchell Slough," said Shockley, who has long been a strong advocate and activist in support of access to the slough. "He's going to be dead and gone and his kids are going to be gone, and that's still going to be a good deal with this state."

Sharpe and the Montana Wildlife Federation were on the front line in a 2007 fight over a bill to codify public access to waterways at public bridges. This particular debate centers on James Kennedy, the chairman of Cox Enterprises in Atlanta. He owns a ranch on the Ruby River in southwest Montana and brought on this battle when he tried to prohibit fishermen from accessing the Ruby River off a public bridge. State attorney general Joe Mazurek ruled in 2000 that the public had the right to access streams at bridge crossings. But the ruling does not exist in the Montana code, and thus is vulnerable.

After the bill failed to get out of committee, Schweitzer included some similar language in an amendatory veto of a bill dealing with state funding of bridge improvements, making the money contingent on public access. The amendment failed, but he had made his point.

Schweitzer said the amendatory veto was important to clarify the attorney general's opinion. It was his prerogative to ensure that counties were only allowed to spend state money on bridges that provided public access. "If a bill comes to me that would abridge the constitutional rights of Montanans, then I have a right to amend it. This is simply saying that we won't use funds to restrict their constitutional rights," Schweitzer told Dan Testa, a reporter for NewWest.Net.

Sharpe applauded Schweitzer for the move. To Sharpe it demonstrated how well the governor understands the importance of protecting Montana's hunting and fishing heritage. "He is a governor of action and he likes to get things done, and while it may have been bold, I think it might have triggered some further discussion that will appear in the near future."

In 2006 Schweitzer also announced the "Square Deal with Montanans," a program that included, among other things, monies allowing the state to buy access sites on rivers that are surrounded by private land or where landowners are resistive to public access. With property values only going up, Schweitzer's program will give sportsmen a chance to secure some access before the land is out of reach. Schweitzer justified the program by saying, "If we're going to assure our residents and nonresidents some opportunity [to hunt and fish], then we need to have access."

Sportsmen in Montana, as well as the rest of the West, are both Republican and Democrat. Courting them makes sense for Schweitzer the politician. But his sportsman persona is also, I believe, a genuine reflection of the man's character. The ads showing him with a fluorescent orange vest and a shotgun are not fictionalized. He's able to talk at length and with authority about what flies catch the most fish on what stretch of stream and what rifle caliber works for elk, and while he may not be the best fisherman ever to pick up a five-weight, he clearly knows what he's doing.

And in his second State of the State speech, he announced that he'd bought his wife, Nancy, a pistol for a birthday present. Not much on the romance scale, but something that made gun owners all around the state smile.

33

Me and Schweitzer

How do you gauge a governor?

I remember sitting in graduate journalism classes at the University of Montana and discussing the notion of authorial bias. Is it appropriate for a reporter to interject his or her own perspective into a piece? The arguments went back and forth, my own position being that, to the extent that you can remove bias, you should. Who cares what I think as a journalist? But when it comes time to judge the performance of an elected official—with all the personal biases that the judgment unavoidably implies—I'm not sure it's possible to remain neutral.

I came to Montana as a conservative. As I progressed through journalism school, however, I found myself turning moderate. By the time I met Schweitzer, I was, and still am, firmly middle of the road. If I had to choose, I'd say I'm an Independent. The last election, if Bob Brown hadn't supported an initiative to repeal the voter-initiated ban on cyanide mining for gold, he would have had my vote. As it was, and based mostly on that issue, I voted for Schweitzer instead. Is he my governor?

Unavoidably, yes. And now, three years into his administration, do I think he's doing a good job?

As I was told several times during the process of researching this book, a governor must first and foremost be able to work with his legislature. Schweitzer's success in this regard is debatable. While he didn't get along with everyone, he did accomplish a number of his priority agenda items. Could he have done more if he'd had a more congenial relationship with the Republicans? Schweitzer's personality probably kept tensions higher than they might have otherwise been (although this isn't to say that the Republican leadership doesn't bear every bit as much of the blame as he does).

One thing I've learned about my own personality is that I tend toward empathy. Interestingly enough, I've seen this most in myself as a journalist. I've covered many controversial issues and people and when I hear a position explained with passion and thoughtfulness, it's hard to keep up the healthy skepticism a journalist must have. I can honestly say that I've never covered an issue that didn't have points on both sides. The same goes with Schweitzer.

He, by his own admittance, makes decisions he thinks are right no matter what interest group or contingent he upsets. He's intelligent and a quick study. When he gets hold of an issue, like all-day kindergarten for example, or prescription drugs, or coal to liquids, he works tirelessly to become enough of a passionate expert to sway people to his side.

Mike Cooney, whom I interviewed about Schweitzer's dealings with the legislature and his performance as governor, is, quite honestly, in awe of the man. Cooney comes from a long Montana political background. Frank Cooney, his grandfather, was the state's ninth governor.

Cooney believes Schweitzer's authentic confidence and intelligence attracts many supporters. "I don't think Brian Schweitzer has invented himself. I think what you see with Schweitzer is the real deal and it's a tremendous fit with whom Montanans are and what they're looking for in their political leader. He's so damn confident."

But the criticisms, particularly from Republican leadership in the house during the 2007 legislative session, were loud and passionate. "Their criticism was based on their frustration of being out of power and facing a very formidable opponent." The same confidence and intelligence that makes Schweitzer a very capable governor, also makes his critics uncomfortable, Cooney said.

Now that I've listened to those who like him and those who don't, I agree with Cooney. Schweitzer's persona is simply who he is. He's not politically polished, though he is politically savvy. He works extremely hard to learn the issues he champions. He's not a man who is likely going to give speeches remembered for generations, but he will be the source of stories and legends in Montana political history.

A governor in Montana must also be available to the constituents. He works for us, after all, and should be answerable to us for his decisions. This is Schweitzer's forte. He's a natural born hand shaker and small talker. Although he's somewhat of a celebrity in the state, it's hard to imagine that he could be any more available to his constituency.

A governor must also be able to handle the media. Schweitzer has made it a point to keep his door open to reporters around Montana and has so far managed to avoid the sort of tiffs that plagued Martz. At first, I was frustrated by Schweitzer's ability to dodge questions and ignore honest attempts to probe his personality, politics, and past. But eventually, things began to change and I have no explanation for it. After months of trailing him around the state, we finally began to have lengthy discussions on his family, leadership philosophy, and governorship. I learned that you have to let him talk. If you call him for a quick quote, he'll give it to you. But if you call him for a lengthy interview, he might take some time talking about everything from cattle genetics, to the media coverage of his dog, before he gets to your questions. Maybe it comes from his time spent in the Middle East dealing with bedouins, as he claimed. Maybe it's just natural. By the end of this project, he'd answered all my questions and often more than once.

When I first met Schweitzer at that campaign rally in Hamilton, I liked him. I liked the way he approached me and just started the small talk. I liked his casual demeanor. But the thing that perhaps impressed me most, from that first meeting, he never forgot my name.

I'd give Schweitzer high marks as a governor. He is partisan at times and I think this brings on the ire of his critics. Not necessarily because of his politics, but because of his forceful personality. But really, that's fine with me. He doggedly promotes Democratic causes around the state, which is what he should do. Of course he's been able to occasionally reach across the aisle—the deals he cut prior to the 2007 special session are a great case in point—but he's obviously and strongly guarded with his Republican peers.

Some critics might say that Schweitzer would get more done if he wasn't so forceful. They may be right. But I would argue that if he weren't as forceful, Montana wouldn't have such a successful promoter. Granted, that promotion of Montana seems to sometimes take a back seat to the promotion of himself and his ideas, but Montana has not had this kind of attention in a long time—maybe ever.

He's good at shaking hands and making friends with reporters. That's a skill as natural to him as breathing. He likes people and it shows. He wants people to like *him,* and it shows. Sometimes, however, Schweitzer is apt to go on and on about himself or one of his ideas and forget that the conversation is a two-way street. Of course, it is obvious he would do this with a journalist. But I didn't always have my notebook out. He's neglected on several occasions to introduce me to his friends or peers. It was rude and a little unsettling, but I eventually figured out that was simply the way he was and it wasn't personal.

He's good at turning the other cheek; at least it looks that way. Sometimes he's too sensitive to personal attacks. In a national arena, surrounded by polarized pundits nightly howling for blood, he would likely need a thicker skin. I do think he wanted to forgive Mike Lange for the YouTube tirade during a 2007 Republican legislative caucus but couldn't completely pull it off. His later comments about the incident point out that he still has little regard for Lange, and that he's still angry. But Schweitzer has told me several times that he is not thinking of a higher office: "At the end of the day I'm going to do this for awhile and then I'm going to go back to being a private citizen and be proud of it." But if he is indeed thinking of politics beyond Montana, he's apt to tackle it with the same intensity that he's approached the governor's office.

As a citizen of Montana, as someone who voted for Schweitzer in the past and has come to know him reasonably well, if I were indeed writing his report card, I would give him mostly A's and a few B's. But next to the line *Plays well with others,* I would have to scribble "needs improvement."

34

Last Thoughts

Esteemed journalist Janet Malcolm, in a controversial essay on the relationship between author and subject, wrote, "In our society, the journalist ranks with the philanthropist as a person who has something extremely valuable to dispense (his currency is the strangely intoxicating substance called publicity), and who is consequently treated with a deference quite out of proportion to his merits as a person."

I did have frustrations with Brian Schweitzer. After a couple of episodes where my interview attempts fell flat—"We'll try again some other time" type of thing—I came away with a bruised ego. He clearly, early on, didn't value the work I was doing. But for every time he was less than hospitable, there were other times when he was familiar, friendly. He joked with a fellow reporter once that his dog was better looking than me, and when he found out I took a break from working on this book to get married and go to Alaska for a late-September honeymoon, he gave me some practical advice. "Start planning a trip south. Maybe the Bahamas. Start planning today." Sometimes he's made me laugh and sometimes cuss.

Schweitzer finally proved to be a difficult subject for a biography. Getting him to examine his own life was like pulling teeth. He was clearly uncomfortable with the whole notion of a biography. I did however finally find a way to get Schweitzer to focus on my book—the telephone. While he's difficult to pin down face-to-face, I could get him to focus in small chunks over the phone. We generally talked early in the morning before he went to the office. In these interviews, as opposed to the sit-down discussions, he was relaxed and open. He answered the questions I had been nervous to ask, like about his being labeled as a bully and about his son Ben. He's never asked to see the book, never once asked what I was finding out about him. To his credit he never probed. He did, however, question me a couple of times as to why the hell I would write a book about him: "I don't know who you think's going to buy this thing."

Do I know the governor any better than I did a year ago? Oddly enough, even after all the interviews, the time spent on the phone, the library research, perhaps the single most insightful thing I've heard said about him came from a friend of mine, someone he'd just met.

In the summer of 2007, I ran into the governor at a function in the Capitol, an exhibit on Sudan. I was with my friend, a pastor in Helena. Schweitzer was there with Nancy. I hadn't come prepared with notebook or recorder, so I didn't approach him to talk. I just figured he'd seen enough of me.

Steve and I were browsing the photographs in the display when I felt a hand on my shoulder. It was the governor, coming over to say hello.

I introduced him to Steve, who, by coincidence, had been at a breakfast that day where Schweitzer had talked. Steve complimented him on his speech.

"Well, I'm not too popular with those folks. I don't think they like me too much," Schweitzer said.

"Really?" Steve asked.

Schweitzer started on a familiar rant, going on to say that the group—Hometown Helena—is Republican and Republicans don't like him. He also said that about half the group were lobbyists. "I have this disdain for lobbyists." He went on to talk about lobbyists, how they think they're the fourth branch of government but don't represent citizens, just moneyed corporations.

Then he said good-bye. Later, as we left the Capitol, I asked Steve's impression of the governor. I wondered what his take was on Schweitzer's frustrated monologue about lobbyists.

I respect Steve for his gentleness, for the wisdom he's gleaned from his years as a church leader. His typically generous response has stuck with me.

Steve didn't see the governor's passionate opinion on lobbyists as a flaw, but instead preferred to look at the bigger picture, taking into consideration Schweitzer's position as Montana's leader, the enormous responsibilities on his shoulders. "He just doesn't seem to be at peace."

About the Author

Originally from eastern Oregon, Greg Lemon moved to Missoula, Montana, in the late 1990s, graduating with a master's degree from the University of Montana's journalism school. He has worked as an environmental and outdoor reporter for the *Ravalli Republic,* as well as an editor for the popular online news magazine www.newwest.net. He lives in Hamilton, Montana.